The Way of the Mile High Maverick

By Stephen Oliver, MBA

The Way of the Mile High Maverick

By Stephen Oliver

Advisor Wealth Mastery

Martial Arts Wealth Mastery

825 Neville Lane, Golden, CO 80401

303-217-3278, FAX 800-795-0583

StephenOliver@AdvisorWealthMastery.com

Other Tools and Resources Available at
www.AdvisorWealthMastery.com

StephenOliver.Financial

StephenCOliver.com

Contents

Preface

Many of the chapters of this book are from confidential high-level letters to my coaching members, or newsletters sent only to members, or rarely, internal correspondence to business owners or staff. Therefore, some will have dated references or references to events happening at the time the memo, letter or newsletter was written. They have been included because the philosophy behind the conversation is 'evergreen' and important for you as a business owner.

I know what you may be thinking:
Who Are You and Why Should I Listen to You?

In the business industry it seems like everyone has popped up to offer advice. How do you tell fact from fiction? Value from fraud? Unfortunately, in business, most of the successful people are spending their time growing their staff, their multiple businesses, and their net profit, but not sharing their secrets with you. I am different from most of those business owners, sharing information in a variety of ways that are important to you and will help you dramatically grow your business and your income.

Many of the "gurus" in our industry fall into one of the following categories:

Never been there — never done that.

There are a lot of people trying to sell you advice who have never sat where you sit and dealt with the problems and opportunities you face every day in your business. Often, they are excellent speakers and persuasive purveyors of their products, services or subscriptions, but they've never done it themselves. Their ideas are unproven, and their perspective is limited to that of an outsider.

Not even a business owner.

Believe it or not, there are 'experts' in business who don't own any businesses. They don't understand the training, mindset, and love for the business community we share — then they dare to tell people who own a business, how to run a business 'the right way'.

They have only run a business in their memory.

Some of those who consult or give expert opinions only run their business in their memory — in some cases that's a distant memory. Some of those recollections seem more like a distant dream (or, in some cases vivid nightmare), and so they aren't giving reliable advice.

Never ran a successful business.

The advice-givers who do own a business, or have run one in the past, typically haven't run a particularly successful operation. Many people began offering advice about running a business only because they couldn't figure out how to make a living running a business in the first place.

"Flash in the Pan"

Often this comes in the guise of "Gee, I just started figuring this stuff out and had a great year last year. How about you pay me to tell you about my short-term successes? I did $ (pick a number $100,000 net, $400,000 gross, etc.) I will do more this year and would love to show you how I did it." Enough said.

Personality driven: not duplicate-able.

I think we'd both be able to draw upon a few examples of 'magnetic personalities' whose personal success is exciting, but not something that could ever be replicated in your operation.

Have lost touch with what works in the 21st century.

Unfortunately, business is full of dinosaurs and leaders of the past, whose time has long since passed, but their friends and associates are unwilling to say: "The emperor has no clothes." Systems that may have been revolutionary in 1970 or 1980 (even 1990 and beyond) may be out of date or just plain insufficient in the present day.

It's Your Choice: Abundance or Lack of Abundance

So, I talked to 10 business owners this week from throughout the United States. Several lamented the economy stating they just aren't great businesspeople and how it's impossible to convince customers to pay or commit to the current economy. I remember one conversation, scheduled for 20 minutes, but the first 10 minutes were spent listening to a very articulate explanation of why it is just impossible for anyone — "but someone like me" — to make a living in the current economic climate.

During the same day, several others told me about how they are hitting records. It's interesting how that works. One business owner said during November and December, he was in the middle of an emotional meltdown — in a panic about numbers and blaming the economy. That same business owner did $45,000 in April, which for him is in record territory — and he is making continuous improvements.

Tony Robbins, on a few of his CDs and during his appearances, talks about "my delusion". What he means is that in many cases, you can choose a belief system about a set of circumstances that either supports your success or your failure. Objectively, neither may be true. If you had the choice of a helpful belief or one that harms you...then, which would you choose?

For instance, you can believe that we are in a marvelously recession-proof industry. You can think it's exciting people are looking to running their own business as an opportunity to feel better, develop their confidence and increase their focus when there's an overall downturn. There's plenty of empirical evidence to support that belief, by the way. During a recession, the movie industry thrives (and they provide their customers with a distraction in the form of entertainment) as well as fitness centers — and liquor stores for that matter. All three are forms of distraction people use.

Let me ask you a question — which belief is more likely to lead to your success: abundance or lack of abundance? This year many businesses are thriving in many different industries. Their business owners and their staff members may be working harder, and they are certainly are working smarter; as a result, their incomes are improving and their profits are up.

There's plenty of opportunity in the current economy, despite what others have claimed. There are possibly more opportunities than ever. Anyway, I'll guarantee you'll get what you expect and see what you believe.

I'm Looking Over Your Shoulder

Before I move on, I'll remind you of a few recommendations I gave — have you acted on them yet?

First Priority: **Organize all possible internal activities and events** that will help to create referrals and add-ons. So, refocus on and master referrals:

- Read one of the books I have recommended (Bob Burg's, for instance).
- Schedule events for clients.
- Celebrate the achievements of your clients, as well as your business.

Schedule crazy internal events regularly — pump it up now. For example, July is 'Anti-Boredom Month' and in July there's 'Cousin's Day'; while the third week of August has been named 'Friendship Week'. Many websites tell you the international awareness days and such. These awareness days, if you use them appropriately over social media and your events, then you can pull more potential customers and investors into your business.

Second Priority: **Make the most of any opportunities you can find to bring in customers and staff.**

- Have a stand at a business expo and talk about your business.
- Attend networking events and functions designed to connect

you to other business owners.

- Have a stand at a job fair or university career event so you can recruit the best members of staff for you.
- Raise money for charity and get out there to help others who are less fortunate.

Third Priority: **A starting point to master referrals.**

The following books are about creating referrals and what I recommend for you to read so you master

referrals. You can easily find them as they are listed at Amazon.com.

- *Endless Referrals, Third Edition* by Bob Burg (Paperback; Oct. 25, 2005).
- *Get More Referrals Now!* by Bill Cates (Paperback; Mar 19, 2004).
- *The Go-Giver: A Little Story About a Powerful Business Idea* by Bob Burg and John David Mann (Hardcover; Dec. 27, 2007).
- *The Referral of a Lifetime: The Networking System That Produces Bottom-Line Results Every Day* (The Ken Blanchard Series) by Tim Templeton, Ken Blanchard, and Lynda Rutledge Stephenson (Paperback; Jan. 1, 2005).
- *Don't Keep Me A Secret: Proven Tactics to Get Referrals and Introductions* by Bill Cates (Paperback; Aug. 27, 2007).

Another Reminder: Back to Basics

What gets measured gets done. Measuring things are a great way to keep track of your processes and analyze what's going well, and what needs to change and adapt. Are you keeping accurate stats of your business' performance? Are you focusing on exactly what's happening and benchmarking with other successful business owners?

Make sure you are keeping accurate numbers on the financial side of your business. Toby Milroy and I have spoken to several businesses, hoping to help them, only to find they had no idea what was happening within their business. It is imperative you have accurate accounting records (profit and loss statements, balance sheets, etc.) and accurate stats every week, month, quarter and year to know exactly how your business and staff are performing. It may seem a lot, but you will start seeing a difference. This is what you should be doing in your business right now.

1. Set Goals.
2. Know your Numbers.
3. Start with the Right People.
4. Develop a Proper Staff Structure.
5. Create a Work-Hard, High-Energy Culture.
6. Ultimately, it's about Marketing and Selling Every Day.
7. Keep your Mission in Mind and What you Are Trying to Accomplish.
8. No Whiners. "Winners Remember Results, Losers Remember Reasons.

#1: You must have a high target or goal for a mid-range objective.

What is the gross revenue, active client count, and net profit levels you want to achieve by the end of the year? What must you accomplish today, this week, and this month to be on track to reach those goals? Every month, set high, but achievable, targets so you are well on your way to completing your end of year goals. Breaking down your huge goals into smaller ones helps to make them seem more achievable. Make sure everyone knows what they must accomplish every day to be on track to reach these goals.

#2: Measure and track everything.

Keep several key measures in your head (and in all your staff members' heads) every day. Focus regularly on improving service, increasing your sales and marketing your product or service. If you don't track your numbers and your ratios, then it's impossible to analyze your results and adapt your processes to improve the results.

#3: Start with the right people.

"You can't teach a pig to sing; it wastes your time and irritates the pig." It's important to hire the highest quality people you can find and create an environment where they can equal or exceed their other career/income opportunities. Choose staff members, not based on solely talent, but on intelligence, drive, charisma and their ability to accomplish your business goals as well as their own goals. If you must supervise the full-time members of staff too much, then you have employed the wrong people. For part-timers and volunteers, it's okay to supervise (and you must) every 15 minutes. Everyone within your team of staff members must look, act and represent company values and the brand. The reason for enforcing hairstyles, cleanliness, a dress code, etc. is to control and help to manage the brand and how it is represented through your employees.

#4: The right staff structure.

It's imperative to have high quality, talented people within every business. The owner-operator, who will be 100% focused on the results of the business is essential. It's imperative to have a full-time person focused on running the business effectively, marketing it and ensuring the client base is growing. It may be important to have another full or part-time person focused on other aspects of the business, like employee wellbeing, finances, and other logistics. Neither of these people can be working a second job; you want their full energy and attention on your business.

#5: Don't create a culture of clock-watchers.

If someone starts complaining about working too many hours or working too hard, then they are the wrong person for the job. The day must be segmented, with time for external promotional activities (business-to-business marketing, group activities, community fundraising, charity events, etc.). Splitting the day up increases the amount of fun you can have in the workplace and leaves behind the culture of clock watchers. Your employees will be driven to learn more and grow more in their role and will have a genuine interest in the business. Set a tone of no excuses and focused goal setting to keep your employees motivated. Involve everyone in making things happen every week. This will motivate them further to put in the maximum effort every day.

#6: The meaning of the saying 'making the rounds of emails' is something to the effect of: "Every day, the antelope wakes knowing it must run faster than the fastest lion to survive. Every day, the lion wakes knowing it must run faster than the slowest antelope to survive."

The business version of that thought — the equivalent within the business world — is marketing. Every day, you wake up knowing you must have 20-plus new customers this month (and every month for the rest of your life) to thrive. There are plenty of marketing systems, ideas and information online you can look at, however, you must start the day with your blank pad and ask: "How much extra will I do today, this week, and this month to make sure I hit the numbers I need to get?" At one end of the spectrum, you can hit the mall with a clipboard and special offers, host big internal events, or run a successful brand awareness campaign. The question is: "Are you running faster than the fastest lion?"

#7: Keep in mind what you are trying to accomplish. Create your company mission. Refer to it daily. Stay on track.

Any obstacles or unnecessary distractions from your primary company mission are potentially destructive, avoid them at all costs.

#8: You can't develop winners if you aren't one.

Ultimately, regardless of all the stuff you can provide for your staff members to help the business, they will look up to you and model their behavior on you, so you need to set the right example. You can't develop "no-excuse" employees if you are full of excuses yourself. You can't develop confident employees if you lack it yourself. Make sure you are a product of the product, every day, in every way. Ultimately, your success is up to you. You work hard, pay attention and follow the system...or not. There's nothing or no one to blame but yourself if you fail to thrive. Every tool you need is available and every support system is in place. The question is "Will *you* choose to be a winner or not?"

Are You a Soldier in the "Alarm Clock Army?"

I've had in-depth conversations with approximately 15 business owners from different industries during the past week. Some are grossing $50,000 to $70,000 a month; two of them are down from $400,000 to $450,000 per year to now $250,000 to $300,000 a year; a few others are in the $6,000 to $10,000 range.

After talking with them and discussing the opportunities and problems of around 30 more businesses, I've arrived at several conclusions about what factors limit business owners of all industries and professions.

Let me start with a quote from an interview with Ted Nugent I stumbled across when I was 17, watching him perform "Cat Scratch Fever" in Tulsa. I never expected to use his words for success quotes! By the way, at that concert, Rush was his warm-up act.

Ted Nugent talks a lot about discipline. Speaking on the phone from his ranch outside Waco, Texas, the Detroit-born guitarist comes back to it again and again. His life of clean living is the way to go, he says, living another way is nothing less than insane. Nugent, who comes to Phoenix Sunday not to perform, but to speak at the National Rifle Association's annual conference, is a conservative. As a member of the NRA's board of directors, he's a gun nut to be sure, but he's also a bow nut, a family nut, an organic food nut, and an alarm clock nut.

"I like to call it the 'alarm clock army'. Those of us that still set our alarm clocks because we have a responsibility to perform, to produce, to be punctual and attentive, and professional and pursue excellence. We come in every shape and form, we come from every walk of life."

I thought it was an interesting quote — "Alarm-Clock Army?"

I think back to another friend (former CEO of a company) who gave me a great quote: "One of my objectives is never to have to wake up to an alarm clock ever again." I had observed, first-hand, this mindset is retiring on the job without telling anyone. The culture then evolves to emulate that

16

behavior. Many of the business owners I have talked to during the last week echo that sentiment in either one way or another. They have mentally 'checked out'. They have hit numbers that put them beyond their comfort zone and then semi-retired on the job. The number doesn't matter, I've seen a range of business owners semi-retiring over various amounts of numbers, from just breaking even to more typically $50,000 to $70,000 a year, and, in some cases, the low $100,000s. Rather than hoping for more and building a better business, a stronger business strategy and a more robust customer experience, they go into semi-retirement.

Immediately, the numbers slip and when that happens, you can usually see the pattern. Guess what most of them do next? They complain about the economy and about the fact they have no money in their budget to advertise more. They complain the economy has negatively impacted their business. All the while, they forgot the "alarm clock." They became lazy and instead of trying to fix the issues, they essentially look for a good excuse to hide behind. How else does this manifest? In many cases, it's by hiring staff and then 'abdicating responsibility for their results'. I can't tell you how many times I've talked with an owner who doesn't know what his director does on a minute-by-minute or hour-by-hour basis. They don't know the tools and marketing campaigns that have been created for use in attracting and keeping potential customers. This certainly isn't a problem that only happens in certain types of businesses, and it's not even a small company problem.

A great story I remember hearing is what happened when Frank Wells and Michael Eisner took the helm of Disney. Eisner brought Jeffery Katzenberg (now of DreamWorks SGK [Spielberg, Geffen, Katzenberg]) with him from Paramount. According to the story, they inherited a 9-to-5 culture, and by Friday early afternoon, all the executives were gone — with many heading to the golf course. Immediately, Katzenberg started scheduling movie production meetings (upcoming script reviews, marketing planning, etc.) for the Disney movie studios on Sunday morning.

Many of those executives who had become lazy left in a huff. However, soon to follow was a string of the studio's biggest hits since Walt died, as well as the launch of Touchstone Pictures and the release of *Good Morning Vietnam* and *Down and Out in Beverly Hills*.

17

Three Deadly Mistakes (and a Bonus Fourth)

A nother big problem I've seen relates to employing staff members. I've been banging this drum for as long as I can remember, but many haven't heard it or haven't gotten it. Business owners tend to do three things that can be fatal to their business.

First, they hire low-quality people. They hire the man or woman who will work for cheap or promote someone who's been the most 'loyal' for many years. It's these owners who experience low results. They hire only from within the company and don't consider outside applicants and the skill sets they could bring to the business. They suffer from what I like to call: "You can't teach a pig to sing; it wastes your time and irritates the pig."

One of my chief trainers at said it recently in a different way: "You can't have mules selling to thoroughbreds." It's an interesting thought. What does that mean though? Your staff have to be a 'product of the product'. They have to set an example of how to be in front of potential and existing customers.

Second, business owners have too much headcount. In other words, they have several part-timers trying to do the work which should be handled by one quality full-time person. This is all well and good, but they're trying to pay for cheap labor, but the job role won't be performed very well. For a business to perform well, it needs two high-quality full-time people; one of these may be the owner. A business also needs a full-time director (typically the owner, in my opinion) and a full-time manager who can help oversee the other members of staff. Therefore, three part-time employees (20 to 30 hours a week) does not equal one full-time person who's focused on results and building his or her income as well as a career.

Third, when business owners find a quality person, they tend to underpay him or her. If someone will work for minimum wage or the lowest end of pay for your industry in your area, then it should be a good indication it's the wrong person. I typically start full-timers at with a base salary decently above the entry level minimum or a percentage of the gross, or whichever is greater. Frankly, if they only earn the base salary more than one or two months in a row, then I'm looking for their replacements. You want people capable of leaning into the percentage of the gross to increase their personal income—people willing to be focused and work hard to accomplish it.

Another deadly mistake of business owners is a failure to recognize the hourly value of their time.

I was talking with a coaching client a couple of years ago. His business was on the lowest rung of what I typically accepted ($12,000 a month gross). He made two statements back-to-back which immediately struck me as silly:

He was frustrated at not being able to break the $12,000-per-month barrier at his establishment, a plateau on which he said they had been stuck before working with me and he urgently wanted to achieve larger numbers.

He also said he was very pleased he had many clients paying $80 per hour for one of his services. This, in turn, made me think, so I paused for a minute before commenting and asked if he had a calculator. After he handed it over to me, I shook my head and asked him to divide $12,000 a month by 4.2 (weeks in a month).

Next, I asked him to divide that number by 40. Upon asking him the total, he said it was a little less than $80. I pointed out obviously he had valued his time at $80 an hour which was approximately the level the business was performing.

Then I asked, "Where would you like to be within the next 90 days?" His response to me was $30,000 a month. Working backward, I explained everything he touched had to be worth $180 an hour if his business was to earn $30,000 a month during a 40-hour workweek. To move to $50,000 a month meant each hour must be worth $300. This was a huge amount of money to set at an hourly rate.

Another business owner, doing a little more than $10,000 a month on average, explained he had taken a $35,000-a-year 'day job' to supplement his income. Well, that translates to $17 per hour. There are many things you can do to make $80, $100, $120, or even $300 or more per hour—if you are working on your business effectively with maximum energy.

Be Aware of Current Trends

If you want to attract potential customers who will come back time and again to buy and use your service and product, then you must be aware of current trends and be consistent with your brand and tone of voice. It's impossible to run a successful business with high-quality services and products while trying to offer the 'latest trends' all the time and keep them at a high standard. That doesn't mean you can't integrate the trends to create high-quality products your customers will want to buy.

Don't miss the point you are always competing for business in your industry. Just because you're unique today, doesn't mean someone else isn't going to 'set up shop' with something very similar to your business tomorrow. Just keep researching your market all the time and find ways to be the best option for consumers.

On a lighter note, I've recently made time for what I truly mean to do on an ongoing basis. What is that? I've been touching base again with some dear old friends and sharing their honest and divergent opinions about our relationships.

Is Your Biggest Challenge Your Attitude and Energy?

As I've reiterated before in this book, while talking with many business owners and dedicated many painstakingly long hours of research and interviews, I've found two common issues limit the owner's success: their attitudes about their lives and businesses, and the energy they expend on their businesses.

My objective is to reveal common denominators which cause business owners to struggle with the way they see and react to the world around them. The title of Wayne Dwyer's book, *You'll See It When You Believe It*, speaks volumes and could turn around many lives if its meaning is understood. And I recommend you try to understand the book's message.

When events in your life create negative feelings or when people with whom you interact with every day leave you frustrated, then it's time to evaluate your belief system. After all, the world around you is just a reflection of your thinking.

Although the term, 'people management' may be inappropriate or the incorrect term, it is a good place to start. As one smart author once wrote: "You manage things; you lead people." Leading people and inspiring them, instead of trying to manage them, creates a better working environment and inspires them to put all their effort into working for the business. Ultimately, they will respect you as a leader, and you will have earned their respect. During the years, I've adopted some meaningful metaphors for feeling frustrated when 'managing people'.

Accomplishing anything in one's life (or business) is like 'pushing rope'. Managing people is like 'herding cats'.

These metaphors may reflect the way you've felt many times, and they also indicate an attempt to manage instead of leading. Pushing people to accomplish tasks, to be more responsible or excel is worse than 'pushing rope' since people will push back or resist your attempts to manage them. In either case, pushing people or herding cats are both highly unproductive and won't get you anywhere.

Like me, I am sure you have struggled with the same unproductive mental cycle — irritation, frustration, anger, and then finally, the realization that the only way to lead your organization is by example.

If you want your sales executive to source more or better clients, then lead by example and show them more efficient ways, and tips and tricks you have learned throughout your career to improve their methods. This is how you can improve your sales efforts as your team will then learn from you teaching them the model for success.

The adage: "do as I tell you, not as I do it" neither leads nor inspires anyone and should be directly avoided. Too many business owners find themselves trapped when they lead from the front when training, but still end up pushing their staff to improve business performance while ignoring it themselves and turning a blind eye. It just doesn't work — and this has been proven time and time again.

Tweaking your systems, writing manuals, or implementing rewards and punishments systems will never fix your failure to lead from the front. Furthermore, if you're assigning staff members to take on the responsibility of managing systems or accomplishing tasks you don't understand yourself, then this is also a similar failure to lead on your part. As the owner of a company, you must master each of the core processes — marketing, sales, finances, and social media — before you hire a new employee or involve a current employee in the management of these processes, regardless of how well those employees may be able to do the job. Sales is a particularly misunderstood and mismanaged process in most businesses. It is not uncommon for owners to feel that selling is beneath them, while never realizing their most important job as an owner is to sell not only the products and services to the customer, but sell the jobs in their business to the potential members of staff and show them they are a fantastic opportunity that will give them great career progression and develop their maximum potential.

Any business person should understand a key mission of their teaching role is to encourage their members of staff to learn new things and progress within the company. There are few of those staff members who would respect a leader who refused to "sell" their products.

23

Never Stop Learning

No matter how much you know, there's always more to learn. How many non-fiction books have you read this year? Do you take notes when you read?

Do you write in the books and jot ideas and implementation strategies?

Do you ever re-read a book 2, 3, 5 or 10 times?

Do you love Amazon.com or your local Barnes & Noble bookstore?

How many biographies have you read?

How many audio CDs have you purchased, and then listened to their contents repeatedly?

Are you on the Nightingale-Conant preferred-customers list?

Do you obtain any industry-specific information that is available?

Do you subscribe to all the helpful business tip websites?

How many DVDs have you purchased and watched?

Do you own the Kovar series?

How many business DVDs do you have?

Do you go to many seminars?

Do you go to every industry-specific seminar?

How much would you spend for a seminar? Would $2,000, $3,000, $5,000 or $10,000 be too much? Why?

What types of seminars would you and have you attended? Is it time to 'learn outside the box' and explore other subjects?

Have you ventured outside of your comfort zone?

Have you thought about returning to college?

Would a BA, BS, MA, MS or MBA help achieve your goals?

Do you have any mentors?

How often do you talk to them?

Do you know their strengths and weaknesses?

How's your peer networking?

Do you talk with at least three people per week who are doing something better than you?

Do you share and obtain ideas regularly?

Do you talk to successful people outside your 'normal' circle of acquaintances?

The most successful people I know do several things religiously:

Read the biographies of successful people.

Read often.

Keep a dictionary on their desks and search for words they don't know or use consistently.

Break from their 'paradigm' to look at things in new ways.

Talk to people who are more successful than they are.

Listen more than they talk.

As soon as you stop learning, you stop growing. Look for new information and always apply it to your business and life. Avoid learning just for the sake of it but apply the information quickly.

The Economy Sucks? Really?

I've had the interesting and simultaneously annoying experience of car shopping recently.

A couple of months ago I was running errands — trying to find copies of *The E-Myth* at various bookstores around Denver since I had waited until the last minute to decide to use the book for our Regional Developer Training. While we waited to turn left into a Barnes & Noble parking lot, an otherwise nice 18-year-old, recent graduate gunned his SUV while looking for songs on his iPod. He failed to notice my car's blinking turn signal and rammed into my Mercedes at probably 35 mph and accelerating.

His SUV looked like it had been in a war. His 'deer catcher's' front end was torn off. Smoke was emitting from the engine. His front bumper was gone, hood crumpled. His SUV wasn't drivable in the slightest. In my case, my Mercedes had a dent in the rear quarter panel; the bumper was unharmed, except the plastic cover, which snapped back into position. Myself, Rob, and the young man waited for the police, and during that time, I consoled the young man. Afterward, I proceeded to purchase a couple more copies of the book and drove to our next errand. Well, the insurance company also totaled my car, giving us approximately $10,000 more than the repair estimate. Mercedes parts can cost more than expected, and some of the electronics can increase the price by a lot. So, now I'm looking for a replacement car of course; I needed it to get to places.

It's interesting because I know those car companies, dealerships, and salespeople have been whining for a year now about how bad their industry has become. Anyway, on to my point. We've been visiting many BMW, Mercedes, and Lexus dealerships, looking for a mid-size, 4-door sedan with an all-wheel drive. As we were looking for a specific type of car, this then narrows the choices down to a Lexus GS 350 AWD, BMW 5-Series (BMW 535ix) and another Mercedes E Series (E500 4-Matic).

After visiting a bunch of dealerships, you would think these guys are semi-retired and really would prefer to collect the cars rather than sell them. What do I mean? Well, Jodi (my now ex), seems determined to get the BMW 535ix. The totaled Mercedes was originally her car; I primarily drove the Porsche Turbo). We went to a huge new dealership in South Denver. It has a huge inventory and a multi-million-dollar facility in a location between Cherry Creek and Highlands Ranch (a rich area of town).

We've been to that dealership three times now. Each time, we've visited, we've dealt with salespeople who did the following:

1. Kept us waiting for what seemed like hours (in reality, we probably waited around 15-20 minutes before being helped by them).
2. Had no idea what inventory they had.
3. Had no idea how the features and functions of the cars they were selling worked.
4. Spent one to three hours with us, including test-drives in at least one car.

After all the above, none of the three salesmen asked for my name, address, phone number or email. No one asked any standard background questions, i.e., what I do for a living or why we were shopping now. None of them even asked what car we wanted specifically so they could find it for us. There was no follow up afterward, and it was clear the company had no system or method in place to follow up with their customers to see if they were interested in a car from their dealership. This dealership must have millions of dollars invested in its facility, huge overhead, and a huge inventory.

Most of the time, its salespeople were hanging out in the dealership (several of them played with my daughter's new puppy during one trip). I'm sure the owners of the dealership were sitting in their offices, bitching about the recession, and worried about the inevitable downturn.

I'm betting he spent 100 times more money on the facility in comparison to the service and sales training for the staff members. Indeed, this was an incredibly stupid move on his part. We needed a new car and we walked into the dealership with a check in my pocket; we were ready to buy. We were as 'live' a prospect as exists.

Anyway, we visited another dealership. The salesperson was a retired chief from the Air Force. He asked background questions and did his best to determine exactly what Jodi wanted (not that I could recognize the difference of the three she hadn't liked. The wood trim on the door was the wrong color or orientation, or some such thing).

This salesperson followed up after we had left the dealership. He researched new and used inventory which was on its way to the dealership. He called whenever a new car was headed for prep, as well as generally built rapport with us, followed up and has essentially done his job extremely well.

I'll tell you sincerely even if it's not exactly the car we wanted, I still wanted to buy it from him. If the other dealership has exactly the right car at the right price, then I'd be disappointed and frustrated to buy it from there.

How does this apply to you?

Well, your customers are more persuaded by your follow-up, sincerity, competence, and care for them than your technical proficiency — certainly more than price. At the first dealership, I'd haggle for every penny. At the second, I'd want to be quoted a reasonable price, but wouldn't be pushing for every penny.

Oh, and at the second dealer, the salesperson has had several cars arrive just this week, and they were sold before we had time to look at them. Recession, what recession?

Several Illuminating Lessons

Allow me to share an email I received from one of the business owners I know:

"I did two sales today that went well; and one Saturday that went to hell. The wife was infuriated with our agreements and wished to terminate. She did some research about your products and services that you provide and was rather irritated that we would like to make money for a living. How in the hell do you respond to that statement? She was ignorant about our products and service, and just frustrated the living hell out of me. Sorry, I just thought I would vent a little."

I want to share this message with you because it provides several illuminating lessons:

First, and, most importantly: You can't please everyone all the time. If you try to please everyone, then the results are inevitable. You mean nothing to anyone. It's important to recognize most personal success stories are polarizing. The successful people tend to be at one end of a spectrum or another, such as Rush Limbaugh and Howard Stern on radio, Donald Trump on TV, or even Bruce Lee.

Anyone who is very successful gains both a loyal following and an opposing group who loathes his or her success. Successful people must realize that offending a segment of the population goes with the territory.

Second: Be immune to criticism. Never, I repeat, never, take rejection personally or worry about what the critics say. My business operator was frustrated and his report to me was full of his raw emotions because he was reacting to the woman's criticisms personally.

I immediately recognized his 'personal' reaction; however, I also realized if his feedback about this dissatisfied customer was even 30% accurate, then we didn't want her in his business. Part of the definition of a professional is the ability to reduce the intrusion of emotions or personal reactions into the decision-making process and operation of your profession.

If movie stars and celebrities did not have this ability (and not all of them do), then they would be emotional wrecks. You must be immune to criticism to be successful, and the more successful you become, the more critics you will attract.

Third: be extremely satisfied with 'two steps forward and one step back'.

You read the email: 'I did two sales today that went well; and one Saturday that went to hell'. Naturally, the owner/operator was allowing his frustration and disappointment about the one bad customer to make it seem more important than the two sales that went well.

Those were easy; full of pleasantries and no spikes of emotion to register sharply on the memory. While the one 'that went to hell' sent emotions off the scale, which is the one most remembered.

The trick is to re-direct your emotions to your successes. Revel in those and forget the rejection. After all, one renewal per business day equals 20 to 25 per month — and I'd be happy with that any month. There's no value to becoming frustrated by one dysfunctional human being, except to learn there will be more!

Fourth: the solution is often 'supply and demand'.

Supply and demand are one of the oldest theories, or laws, of economics, and it applies to your business, regardless of size, in much the same way as the largest global corporation. Understanding supply and demand and using it advantageously will solve many problems operating your business.

In simplest terms, you win when what you supply is limited, but there is a great demand for it. If you have a huge surge of new customers, then several positive results occur, for example, fewer people complain. Furthermore, you are less concerned about clients who 'don't fit' with your business's culture. You reduce the need to sell because the trust and credibility of your 'social proof' begin to dominate prospects' decision-making, which makes them want to be involved with your business.

Multiple Businesses, Licensing, and Partnerships

I've been inundated recently with questions from Coaching and Mastermind members and others about opening multiple businesses through license agreements, partnerships, or various other 'business agreement' scenarios. There was also an article in an industry magazine which addressed this topic, and I believe the author was partially right but suggested dangerously wrong conclusions.

Those who have been asking me about how to expand your business into multiple businesses are contemplating what amounts to a franchise business without complying with franchise law. That is a risky and, frankly, an unwise move.

This is a subject in which I've become an expert during the last four or five years. I'm an American Bar Association member, a member of the ABA's forum on franchising and an International Franchise Association member. I've also provided the means for the law firm that represents my interests to live in opulent style for the past several years, helping me to register as a legitimate franchise business.

The International Franchise Association recently estimated $250,000 to $500,000 is required for a new franchisor to open their doors, and the franchisor failure rate is approximately 70%. Having been through the process from A to Z, I don't question either number; it is quite accurate.

The rationale for an entrepreneur to become a franchise business owner is undeniable, as the following excerpt from a recent article confirms:

"A good way to reduce your risk of failure is to purchase a franchise because franchises typically have a higher success rate than other types of small businesses. Conventional wisdom holds that franchises have a failure rate of about 5 percent, compared to the 50 percent failure rate of independent entrepreneurs. Successful franchisors have developed 'formulas' for starting a new

31

business. Good franchisors want your new business to succeed. If you fail, they fail."

I receive enough returned mailings and general correspondence to know the failure rate of independent businesses far exceeds 20% per year, which is 100% in 5 years; and doesn't include what I call the 'walking dead'. Another article excerpt will reinforce my point.

"This is the franchise duck test: if you act like a duck, look like a duck, and talk like a duck, then you are a duck. Even if the duck advisor, i.e. your attorney, says you are a cow. You can't do business legally as a cow if you are a duck. More importantly, you don't get to vote! Franchising is regulated by law.

"The general test of whether or not a business opportunity is a franchise can be summarized as follows:

If you sell a business opportunity to any person and you:

- Allow the buyer to use your company name or logo
- Charge a fee to the buyer (inside or outside of product or service)
- Provide any significant assistance or maintain any significant control over any part of the business."

I strongly urge you talk to me first, if you are contemplating multi-business expansion. I remain convinced the best expansion process involves on-site ownership with 'residual income' for your efforts as the owner.

Further Thoughts on Businesses

I just spent a couple of days here in Evergreen, Colorado with my old and dear friend, Tim Kovar. Tim has been out of the business for a while now (about two years). He left a company as they added outside management and as the company grew by leaps and bounds, they brought in several million in outside venture capital. It was fun and exciting to catch up with my old friend. It was also interesting to hear his take on the current state of the business industry and a few private thoughts on his business development inside and outside the industry.

He and his brother may join us at our next event. If Tim joins us, then it will be to share ideas about alternative income sources as a business owner. In his case, he has become very experienced in real estate development as well as complementary businesses. I'll relate a conversation I had with Tim many years ago.

He told me his brother, with whom he ran a business, was concerned that something trending in the business world would be the death of traditional businesses generally. When I asked what Dave meant, Tim explained that as people began to rely on technology more, the less they require people or members of staff to do it for them.

At the time, as you may imagine, I told Tim I thought it was crazy.

Despite the advancement of technology, I told Tim, businesses are always going to need employees to help manage things. He believes if this becomes the case, some of his businesses won't be needed and so they'll have to close because they aren't making any money.

I said to him if they thought it was true, they should do a test and survey their customers to see if they preferred interacting with humans during the transactions or deal with technology.

This is one specific example within the business industry, where you have to be aware of the changes within the industry and how they affect your business. If there is a decline in one of the services you offer within the industry, running surveys and tests can help to determine whether you should remove that service or product from your business.

What Is Your Professional Education Worth?

Recently, I've received several comments about the cost of professional education products. Most of their messages can be encapsulated into:

"Gee, all of this stuff is expensive. I can't afford to spend so much."

I even had one old friend who said:

"I'm gaining 10 clients a month and grossing $30,000 a month. I need to reach 20 clients a month and I've been told you are the best in the business industry at marketing. Tell me what I need, and I'll get it."

The conversation was completely undone when my first suggestion received the following response:

"That's too much."

Keep in mind, in his case, increasing clients from 10 to 20 per month generate $30,000 a month or $360,000 per year in added revenues. An even more important consideration is that $360,000 is added revenue per year probably increases his net from $70,000 per year to approximately $400,000 per year — a 500% to 600% *increase*.

The conversation finally ended when my least expensive suggestion, costing approximately $1,200, was countered by his willingness to invest no more than $600.

If you know me at all, then you're able to guess my attitude. I'm still driving my Porsche and he's still gaining 10 clients a month. It's 'no skin off my nose'. It's his loss, and it makes no difference whatsoever to my lifestyle or outlook. I am only able to help those business owners who want help and are willing to invest in their professional education.

How much are you investing in your professional education? I recommend two strategies:

First, you must be willing to invest one dollar if it returns two or more dollars. I often rail on this subject, but I do believe in the Benjamin Franklin quote: "Empty your purse into your mind and your mind will fill your purse."

Second, you should have a continuous study project to help you develop new and existing skills constantly. There are many courses to choose from, but my past course of study may help you choose the one best for you:

- *Educational Psychology*
- *The Psychology of Motivational Teaching*
- *Direct Response Marketing*
- *Internet Marketing*
- *Effective Personal Selling*
- *Rapport Building in Communications*
- *NLP — Applied to Teach*
- *NLP — Applied to Persuasive Copywriting*
- *NLP — Applied to Effective Personal Selling*
- *Direct Mail*
- *Leadership*
- *Employee Management and Supervision*

Let me help you focus on the decision-making process. We'll assume you are already furthering the mastery of your current skills, so then turn your focus onto your business skills, as these skills probably require the most attention. I propose there are three primary skills you must develop to succeed in running your own business.

- *Selling*
- *Marketing*
- *Teaching (your employees)*

Once you begin mastering those subjects, you then must move to staff and master subjects, such as recruiting, hiring, training, supervision, and motivation. If you have decided to grow your career, then where do you start?

First, acquire, read and study the information available from all the great industry sources, including reviewing and ask about my Extraordinary Marketing and Coaching programs, which have a wealth of knowledge about marketing and sales. Aside from that, when I joined Jonathan Mizel's Internet Marketing Coaching Program and Dan Kennedy's Coaching Program, the first thing I did was print everything available on their websites (more than 2,000 pages each). I then organized the material in notebooks and read everything and took notes; I was very determined to learn. These professional education suggestions only scratch the surface of what's available in the industry.

Once you've exhausted all the industry sources specific to your business, then start with generic topics, such as selling and marketing. I recommend:

- *Selling:* Tom Hopkins, Zig Ziglar, Robert Cialdini, and Dan Kennedy.
- *Marketing*: Dan Kennedy and his Magnetic Marketing & Copywriting Programs (visit www.KennedyCopy.com.), Joe Sugarman, John Caples, Claude Hopkins, and others.

Your head may hurt, but great knowledge doesn't come easy. Take your time, organize it all and take one step at a time. My coaching experience with Dan Kennedy, Jonathan Mizel, and others has paid huge dividends.

Success Is Never a Straight Line

With 37 years in business, I feel old! In my day-to-day conversations with business owners generating as little as $6,000 a month and as much as $1,000,000-plus per year, I'm continually reminded of both my arbitrary line to the target and the typically tumultuous line to the top for most successful business people.

I have always been a huge fan of reading biographies, autobiographies, interviews with, and profiles of, successful people — as well as books which analyze and describe the route to success for many millionaires, billionaires, successful politicians and scientists. It's obvious when you read about just about any successful person — from Howard Hughes and Walt Disney to Ray Kroc to Steve Jobs and Bill Gates — that no one had an uninterrupted 'straight-line' to success.

Many forget Steve Jobs, just a few years ago, as Apple's co-founder, was fired by the board of directors and universally reviled inside and outside the company. Now? He's the genius behind Pixar, the largest single shareholder of Disney, and is the genius behind 'Apple's return', including iTunes, the iPod, the return of the Macs, and the iPhones.

How about Donald Trump? A favorite quote of his would-be this, which he said to Marla: "Marla, see that bum on the grate — he's $300,000,000 richer than I am."

Marla said: "How can that be — he doesn't have anything?"

Donald said: "That's right, he has nothing — I'm $300,000,000 in the hole."

Now? He's back on top as the President of the United States. However, it's important to remember that success is not a straight line. During the last year to 15 months, many businesses have closed their doors, while others have learned the economy has changed so much, they must implement a different set of business systems and rules to survive which, in turn, has led to huge growth despite the recession.

Those who have stumbled have received the same universally, repetitive speech:

It's not as bad as it looks; it's not nearly as bad as it feels; stay focused on 2, 3, 5, and 10-year objectives; decide where you want to go and start working.

Those who have had success have typically received the following usual feedback: *It's now time to expand your thinking to the next level; decide how you want your life to unfold and create your business to fully support that direction.*

In some cases — a business owner who was making $30,000 net a year ago, is making that much in a quarter now and in some cases, they are making it in just one month; that's a big change in lifestyle they need to recognize. It's time for an expansion of thinking to move to the next level of success. Where do you go from here?

I'd like to suggest you pick a success study project. One that might be useful is to read biographies or to read one of the books out there which will help you with understanding the successful person's personality.

Some suggestions of these types of books include:

- *Profiles of Power* and *Success: Fourteen Geniuses Who Broke the Rules* by Gene N. Landrum
- *Profiles of Genius: Thirteen Creative Men Who Changed the World* by Gene N. Landrum

Furthermore, here are my suggestions for great business biographies to read:

- *Pizza Tiger* by Thomas Monaghan
- *McDonald's: Behind the Arches* by John F. Love
- *Hard Drive: Bill Gates and the Making of the Microsoft Empire* by James Wallace and Jim Erickson
- *iCon Steve Jobs: The Greatest Second Act in the History of Business* by Jeffrey S. Young and William L. Simon
- *Accidental Millionaire: The Rise and Fall of Steve Jobs at Apple Computer* by Lee Butcher
- *Citizen Hughes: The Power, the Money and the Madness* by Michael Drosnin
- *Pour Your Heart into It: How Starbucks Build a Company One*

Cup at a Time by Howard Schultz
- *Walt Disney: The Triumph of the American Imagination* by Neal Gabler

I'll leave you with a goal statement written by Bruce Lee in 1969. This can apply to the general business industry as well as his industry:

> *"My Definite Chief Aim:*
> *I, Bruce Lee, will be the highest-paid Oriental superstar in the United States. In return, I will give the most exciting performances and render the best of quality in the capacity of an actor. Starting in 1970, I will achieve world fame and from then onward till the end of 1980, I will have in my possession $10,000,000. Then, I will live the way I please and achieve inner harmony and peace."*
>
> BRUCE LEE, JANUARY 1969.

Business Knowledge Aggressively Implemented Produces Awesome Results

We just returned from an academy event in beautiful San Antonio, Texas. Currently I'm prepping for a long weekend of staff and business owner training in Breckenridge, Colorado this weekend.

The Extreme Success Academy was incredible from start to finish. Toby Milroy, Jeff Smith, Bill Clark, Dave Kovar, Terry Bryan, and Keith Hafner are always fantastic. A relatively last-minute addition was Karl Mecklenburg, former Denver Bronco NFL player, who was a six-time All-Pro and played in three Super Bowls. I must say, for me at least, he was the surprise highlight of the weekend.

I've spoken with many of the participants, both during the event and since. There's been a universal agreement this event was much better than last year — and the best event ever, in terms of focused content and a real action plan to implement success.

On another, similar subject, I received this email (edited for space) today.

"I've had a business for more than 16 years. The last five have been very unproductive. My biggest problem to overcome is getting the phone to ring. I have used various marketing materials in the past, with little to no results. The ads are awesome, but interest in them is not.

The bottom line is that I want my business to grow. You provide the resources to make it happen. Let's test the system. Give me an ad with the offer that was very successful with another business; I'll duplicate the process, and then let's see my results.

I am aware that it isn't all about acquiring new clients, but this is number one on my hit list. If I can't cause the phone to ring or drive prospects to my website to schedule an appointment, then the rest of your marketing ideas for retention are irrelevant."

Jeffrey Whitney

I must say it's a shame Whitney didn't attend the event. He would have heard Keith Hafner's spectacular presentation on generating new clients a few years ago. He explained about community outreach rather than one letter or ad slick. He would have heard Bill Clark, Dave Kovar, Jeff Smith, and I discuss how the market has changed and what you must do to run a successful business.

Several of my businesses have generated 50 to 100 new clients during the last 30 days, through community outreach activities, not paid advertising or a one-off ad slick. During the 1980s and 1990s, I could just pour money into newspaper ads and saturation-bombing direct mail and do perfectly fine. Those times have long since passed, especially with the rapid growth of technology.

Learn the Skill of Scanning

The first 'secret' of the skill of scanning is that it's unnecessary to read, study, understand, and master every topic. Instead, find the one good idea which will enhance your operations every month in one of the three key areas: sourcing clients, client retention, and renewals.

I know I've increased the discussion from one good idea to three key operational areas of your business, but I am confident you're still able to follow. When you scan the materials, you only need to look for one good idea which will improve any one of these three key operational areas. Please note, you don't need one good idea for each.

I recommend you try the following steps to scan and absorb the best material which will help you with your business:

- Make copies of the written materials.
- Scan each document and use a highlighter to note anything that catches your attention as a potentially good idea to improve those three areas. It may be a subhead of one of the sections within the text, a statement in the opening paragraph and/or points in the review section. Information presented as bullet points, numbered lists or in boxes is often where a good idea resides.

It will only take you a few minutes of your time to scan even the longest document because you are only looking for the key points to highlight. As soon as you start scanning the documents, you'll notice suddenly you've found a few useful words and phrases from the long documents that have thousands of words combined.

Listen to the audio version next and take notes on how the high points you marked on the transcript are presented and discussed by the contributors. If the contributors provide additional information that will help you understand and implement any of the one good idea you highlighted on the written materials, then you should pause the audio to take extra notes. Furthermore, watch the video and use the same procedure above to find those your good idea.

After you've finished with the audio and video, return your attention to the written material and read and study just those sections, paragraphs, phrases, etc. you highlighted. You may have to read some text before and after your highlighted text to understand it fully, but you don't have to read the entire document to find a good idea or two.

Next, listen to the teleconference and learn how other business owners are implementing their one good idea they found in previous months' materials. Try this scanning method a few times, and you'll quickly discover how little time you need to invest in reading and understanding large amounts of materials.

Remember, you want to avoid empty knowledge; what I mean by this is the knowledge you gain simply to be able to state you know it. Instead, you want to find and absorb a few key concepts that will help move your business to the next level. What is also truly remarkable about this scanning method is the documents you scanned so quickly can be read and studied further in the future to extract other good ideas. It's like having a gold mine you can visit whenever you want to mine another nugget.

This is what I call the 'circling-back' experience. As you use this scanning method more and more, you'll find yourself circling back to key knowledge areas to add to your understanding. Every time you do so, you're adding another layer of knowledge and continuing to strengthen your foundation for greater growth.

In my case, I started with technical business skills and then moved to teaching and instructional skills. Before opening my first business, I worked to master direct-response marketing and selling. From there, I moved to higher levels of skills training, and then extensive educational psychology. I then 'circled back' to sales and sales processes and developing my knowledge further as a result. I circled again to direct-response marketing for even more knowledge about the topic.

This is also a strategy you should use with every material you're learning from. If you continue to circle back to increase your knowledge of the three key operational areas above, then you'll learn more, intensify your level of understanding and mastery of the various subjects and grow more as a person and business professional.

Don't be stressed about reading, or even understanding, every single bit of information; it's unnecessary.

I do want you to be stressed about adding just one good idea or strategy from each package which will make an immediate and positive impact on your business. Of course, that's hardly stressful at all, considering I've shown you how quick and easy it is.

How Would You Know If You "Lost Your Mind?"

L ast week wasn't the best week. I returned from an annual business retreat in Breckenridge, Colorado, where more than 500 business owners attended. Several new businesses joined us this time and there were many tremendous success stories. Owners from throughout North America were in attendance and Jeff Smith, our Regional Developers, and I conducted operations training all weekend. It was truly an uplifting experience (and all at 9,000-foot elevation).

A couple of days later, we had approximately 10 business owners in training for the week, which was when Denver was hit by a massive blizzard. Next thing I know I'm headed home after being stuck on I-70 in our new BMW just as an ambulance pulls into my driveway with EMTs looking for the baby who's not breathing.

The next couple of hours were hair-raising. My 18-month-old son was transported in the ambulance to the hospital in a blizzard. Mom was in the ambulance; I'm following in our SUV (Volvo XC-90 the 'Soccer Mom' Mobile). I didn't know how scary it was until I arrived at the hospital. Chase did stop breathing in the ambulance. I walked into the emergency room with what looked like the entire hospital staff hovering over my terrified son who was screaming. Two days in the hospital and numerous visits from doctors, he was fine but undiagnosed. It was a combination of asthma and allergies which caused him to have difficulty breathing and to stop breathing on the way to the hospital.

Now, I've had tough days, months, and weeks before, but nothing tops following an ambulance with your 18-month-old in it in a blizzard. I was trying not to slide into the ambulance or become stuck on the way. I then walked into a scene from the television show ER, with my screaming baby at the center. I've always been great at handling a crisis, so the effect didn't hit me until Friday or Saturday (Wednesday was the ambulance run, so it was a few days later). In the meantime, during some downtime at the hospital, I made the mistake of checking my email. I discovered a little war of words was actively in progress for a couple of days: an old friend of mine who seems to have finally lost his mind.

Toby sent an email, sharing a couple of ideas Bill Clark presented at the event in San Antonio. Tom Callos had a meltdown from Hilo (HI) which resulted in blog posts, emails, and a raft of back and forth between him and Toby. I always hate to 'swing at pitches in the dirt', but the whole thing became ridiculous. Tom starts calling out everyone involved, including myself, saying we were unethical, underhanded, and teaching concepts (remember this was a shorthand explanation of Bill Clark's idea, and not our idea directly) that are "beneath the dignity of" a business owner.

It's a terrible thing when you lose your mind. For obvious reasons, I didn't intervene other than to send Tom a short note that he really should (and does) know me better after 20 years and he might think before 'flaming'. He did, after flooding the Internet with this, apologize to me.

With all that aside, what's beneath the 'dignity' of a business owner? I certainly believe being broke is beneath the dignity of any business owner. I believe you should do nothing that creates exposure but hurts your image at the same time. For example, things like The Jerry Springer Show, guest passes distributed at a strip club or liquor store, etc....it's a long list. However, most business owners sit on their asses and do nothing. Rather than risk going too far, they do nothing, which isn't the answer either.

I'd equate all business owners to be "raging thunder lizard evangelists" for the value of training in business. The marketing concepts I've typically taught include everything from websites and search engine optimization to direct mail, television infomercials and community outreach ideas; basically, it was anything that could be presented to 300 to 3,000 people at once. I prefer 'high-leverage' activities to one or two at a time. However, rather than sit at your desk in the office and bemoan your lack of results, it would be better to go door-to-door, stand in the cold and talk to people, ask them for feedback in the city center, or distribute offers and discounts at the shopping mall.

Tom, in his misplaced indignity, missed the point that the majority of business owners don't do anything. Those who are growing rich have one thing in common: 'massive action'. They also share another common trait,

46

which is 'taking the credit or the blame for their results', rather than looking for someone or something to blame.

Unfortunately, too many people who advise in the industry aren't running profitable businesses. Some never have; for others, it's been a *long* time since they have. Trust me when I say my objective for you is success most easily and efficiently, but it's not 'magic pixie dust'. You must wake every morning, go to work, and work hard.

Winners Remember Results...Losers Remember Reasons. Which One Are You?

I was in Atlanta a few weeks ago for an event with Dan Kennedy, Bill Glazer, Lee Milteer, George Foreman, and others. Several business owners have taken my advice to pay attention to what Bill and Dan have to say. A couple of them foolishly missed the Academy event, and it probably would have done them *much* better — for those who were at both, congratulations for bettering yourselves.

One speaker was my friend Lloyd Irvin; it was interesting to hear Lloyd speak. Throughout his presentation, he continued to talk about this genius businessperson who started him on the path to becoming a millionaire. He spoke of provocative emails received and about comments made, such as 'any idiot can run a business doing $30,000 or more per month', and other bits of advice he had been given when he was running a $7,000-a-month business that propelled him to make $1,000,000-plus.

Interestingly, I was the genius he meant. Frankly, in my state of mind at that event, my reaction was erroneous: "Gee sounds like I used to be pretty smart." This was not great self-talk; however, it was incredibly interesting to hear my advice filtered through Lloyd to the crowd (and to several staff members and me in attendance).

He explained how he had spent $397 for a 'password' meaning my Digital Extraordinary marketing book and how that book, while he was in Brazil training, pushed his gross from $7,000 to $20,000-plus. He then described paying $2,750 for the first Marketing Boot Camp, and then $5,000 for a 'box of marketing stuff' I was selling at the event. Each time he invested, his return was 100 times or more in his financial results.

Those were his first steps to creating a $1,000,000 business and, quite frankly, a $10,000,000-plus 'marketing empire' that includes running your own business and applying marketing online in the digital age.

He reminded me I had told him unfortunately 97% of people who attend a seminar, read a book, or learned a bit of material, would do nothing with the knowledge. Another piece of advice he shared was the moment I had asked him: "What are your goals for the next 12 months, 3 years and 5 years?" When he answered he hadn't thought of his goals, I responded with a sarcastic: "That's OK, 97% of the people haven't thought about them either — those that won't do anything."

He called what I had taught him the 'secret room'. In other words, others would think you went to a seminar or event and a few of those attendees were taken to a 'secret room' and given the 'real secrets'. Obviously, at the events he attended, which made him a millionaire, *there was no secret room*. He heard the same message from me as others did. It's just that he violently executed it instead of what the others did, which wasn't a lot.

His metaphor, taken from a conversation on a tape that I gave him (sold him) called *The Go-To Guy* by John Carlton and Gary Halbert, is a "gun to the head". Implementing as if someone has a gun to your child's head, and if you don't do it during the time allotted, then your child will be shot.

Most of us act as if tomorrow is as good as today. Big winners take actions that absolutely *must* happen this minute — as if there was a gun to their heads or their children's heads — and they will implement *right now*.

It's what used to frustrate me the most about the bottom one-third of my coaching clients. We'd have the same conversation every month. I'd give them a list of tasks, and then 30 days later they would still not have implemented them. A couple of years ago I chose not to accept coaching clients I thought would be like that and fired those coaching clients with whom I ever had the conversation the third time or if I had many conversations a second time.

What's the takeaway from this? Implement as if your life depended on it. Wake every morning and knock off your top 5 or 6 items on your to-do list. Do them and move forward — *quick*!

The 10 "Secrets" of Leadership

There are many effective styles of leadership, probably, as many as there are different personality types of employees and bosses. That having been said, I do believe there are several secrets to leadership in any organization and becoming a better leader overall.

Vision

You must have a clear and compelling vision for the future of your organization. These are not benchmarks, targeted gross revenue or active customer count, but something much more powerful than these. Your vision is a picture of where you want the organization to progress. It's the bigger picture of how your business should look, described and planned in as much sensory-rich detail as possible. Leadership starts from within. If you have a clear picture of the future of your organization, then your conversation, actions, and goals will tend to fall in line with this vision, and, ultimately, manifest it.

Communication

On the other hand, having a clear vision of the future is valueless unless you become exceedingly effective at communicating that vision to others. That does not mean you must be a gifted public speaker. Many great leaders (including Thomas Jefferson, among others) were not gifted speakers. You may communicate your vision through pictures, public speeches, written communications, or any type of media, but your message must be received by its intended recipients in the most compelling way possible.

Emotional Commitment

You must lead people from their hearts and not their heads. Daily commitment comes from an emotional attachment to the leader, mission, vision, or the target feelings conveyed by your vision of the future. All leadership is based upon the emotional commitment of the followers much more than an abstract intellectual understanding of goals and objectives. Committing to the emotional attachment portrays you as a compassionate leader, who understands their employees are human and embracing it will earn you more respect.

Values-Based

Although financial rewards help motivate or maintain motivation, ultimately, people will wake early and work late with the highest levels of intensity to contribute to others and the community. If financial rewards are directly tied to personal contribution to others, then motivation will remain high. Long-term motivation in any win-lose environment is nearly impossible. Be clear about your overriding values and operate daily within those espoused values.

Congruence

Your words and actions must be congruent. You cannot motivate people to contribute and encourage them to believe in a higher purpose if, ultimately, your integrity is questionable. Although business owners, managers, and politicians have attained high levels with questionable integrity, I maintain long-term leadership must be based upon honesty and the highest integrity. If your manager co-opts your help to hide his extramarital affairs, then how much trust will you give him? If your boss has a different persona in public than in private, will you trust his or her communications with you are sincere?

Team Orientation

Someone once said, "You can accomplish anything if you don't care who receives credit for it." In business, this attitude is exceptionally rare. Many senior business owners have started to believe their press, and act as if anything good that happens to them was their idea. They should give credit, involve the entire team as much as possible to accomplish new directions through consensus. It's better, as the leader, to play a supporting role in many discussions and let the team members find the means to accomplish the ends in your vision.

Results Orientation

Focus on results, not the process it takes. Create accountability from every team member for the result, not the activity. Many ideas are good if implemented effectively. The greatest idea will fail if it is implemented poorly. Allow people, within limits, to choose their means to achieve your agreed-upon end. Manage, based upon results, not activity.

Goals

Once you've implemented all the other 'secrets', establish daily, weekly, monthly, quarterly, and yearly goals. Make sure they are all congruent with your mission, values, and vision. Peter Drucker once said, "What gets measured gets done." Keep records and statistics on everything in your business, but focus on two, three, or four key numbers, and then watch them like a hawk. Graph them, post them in your office, at the reception desk, in the employee break room, or even at the front door of the office. Nothing motivates action like a huge graph of your targeted active client count in plain view. Look at your key numbers daily or even hourly to maintain focus.

Walk Your Talk

I know this is redundant, but nothing fails to motivate employees more than hypocrisy. You should decide to live by your values and to be who you say you are 365 days a year, 24 hours per day, 7 days per week.

Fairness

Ultimately, everyone must benefit from the success and suffer from failure — and you do go through both. In compensation, reward people greatly for successes, and make sure there are consequences for failure. If you delegate authority, then focus on the team and allow its members to be 100% responsible for their outcomes. Be supportive, but not paternalistic. If you never allow anyone to fail, then you've never allowed him or her to achieve much either.

Are you a "Raging Thunder Lizard" Evangelist?

I t's fascinating to me the number of creative business owners who live for their arts but are bashful about sharing the value of their art with others. Hopefully, that's not you.

Frankly, if what you do has an incredibly positive, life-changing impact on not only yourself, but everyone around you — especially your staff members and customers—then don't you owe it to *everyone* in your community to show them, convincingly, what it is you offer and the value of your product for them?

Marketing, or publicity, is just communications with the people in your community. You can purchase advertising (print, broadcast, direct mail, etc.) or you can communicate for free (publicity). You can be a speaker or teacher to affinity groups (college, networking events, job fairs, etc.) and introduce your business to large numbers at once or you can be a telemarketer or door-to-door salesperson and introduce your business to individuals one at a time.

You must have a great product, however, and be a true believer (and your staff should be too). You must be passionate about sharing the value of your program with everyone willing to listen. So, how do you convince people in your community the products and services you provide as part of your business are really valuable?

Rule Number 1: 'Long-form' communication is better than 'short-form', which means a one-hour live presentation is better than a 30-second live presentation. On television, 30 minutes (or 27:30) is better than 30 seconds. By mail, a 20-page letter or large package of information, with a DVD or CD, is better than a postcard. A series of presentations are better than one presentation. The more information you can convey and the longer you keep your audience listening and attentive, leads or prospects engaged, the more opportunity you have to 'make your case'.

Rule Number 2: In-person communication always trumps broadcast communications. For instance, if you have a choice of a prospect visiting your website or talking to you in person (by phone or at your office), then in person is almost always *much* better. If you have a choice of prospects (or potential customers) receiving an email or you call them, then the call will be more effective. If you have a choice of talking to them live or them receiving a 'robocall', then in person is always better.

Rule Number 3: A 'participation' event is *always* better than a 'demonstration', with clients as 'spectators'. In all cases, convincing customers to participate and keeping them engaged will always trump passive observation, especially when you're showcasing a new product or offering discounts.

Rule Number 4: Even if a prospect is not interested *today*, it doesn't mean he or she won't be interested next month, quarter or year. You always want to obtain contact information from all 'spectators', 'potential clients', and 'interested parties', so then you can constantly and repetitiously follow-up (you must do this). Email your lead list weekly or daily. Mail information to your potential customers monthly, or more often; call them quarterly, or more often; send them invitations to events or activities. Without contact information, you will obtain a *very* small portion of customers, in comparison to the ones you could get if you maintained frequent contact, which leads to more customers buying from your business.

Rule Number 5: 'Farm your community'. Remember, your community is always changing. Individuals are getting married, divorced, and moving to and from your community. Couples are having kids and their kids are growing, developing, and evolving. Adults and families are sometimes rich and sometimes broke (and typically someplace in between). Sometimes they are bored; sometimes overwhelmed. During some months, certain members of the community will experience trauma which moves them to explore new activities or buy new products. Others will experience trauma which moves them to withdraw from buying things. You must be constantly in front of as many people as possible and as often as possible, so you stay at the forefront of their minds. While you may need to expose them to your message seven-nine times before they pay attention, you must also place your message in front of them when *they* are *receptive*. That means you must constantly and repetitiously generate leads, mail them and call them, and constantly return to the same community of people to reinforce your business and brand.

Rule Number 6: You must 'do enough stuff'. For some businesses, it's as simple as doing more things. Most business owners underestimate the effort and expense to attract new customers. If you are bringing in five customers a month and you need to bring in 20, then it may be as simple as doing four times as much (time and energy or spending). Never discount the fact you just may not be doing 'enough stuff' to generate the results you need. There is no 'Magic Pill'. You may just need to work harder or invest more money in your business, or both to generate those results to keep your business afloat.

Get Off Your Ass!

In a special report in January, I outlined the 10 things you must do to thrive this year. It was a very valuable and important outline of the steps necessary in today's environment to grow your business and have a dramatic impact on your employees, your customers, and your community.

Hello Stephen,

The "10 Things You Must Do to Thrive" was spot on! I couldn't agree with you more and I wanted to tell you. If only more business owners would understand number one!

Anyway, I wish you every success and all the best to Jodi, Jaeda, and Chase.

Buzz Durkin

In addition to being one of my oldest and dearest friends, Buzz is one of the top business owners in the United States. He runs one of the most solid, highest quality businesses I've ever seen. In a small community, he maintains a large client base with the strongest customer retention I've ever seen. He embodies true concern for his customers and a deep reach into his community. Here are the 10 Things I shared which sparked Buzz's enthusiastic response:

Number 1: Premium Pricing is the Quickest Route to a High Net.

Know your value and price your products and services accordingly. We are not in a world where low-price buys a market share. In almost all cases all low prices do is limit your revenue per customer and convince your customers of your limited value. "Absent other criteria, price determines the perception of value." Therefore, it is best to do your research and focus on the pricing list you'll need. It'll come in handy when establishing your worth and finding how potential customers view it.

Number 2: Focus Internally First.

Take out a blank legal pad and focus on what you can do to improve the customer's perception of value. Value starts with rapport. Hire only sincere and honest people who truly care about the customer experience more than their own. By constantly being in contact with your audience, and going to public events, your rapport will build, and so will your reputation and in their eyes, more trust.

Number 3: Have a Strong Sales Process in Place.

Have a strong introduction to your business in a place that answers all their queries about the company, then talk about the 'behind the scenes' of your products, their concept, inception and how they benefit the customer. Implement a focused system to support the process as well as vigorously train all staff on the system continuously so they know it inside and out. Some websites provide extensive training on all sales and marketing processes as well as comprehensive programs.

Number 4: What gets measured gets done.

Keep complete operations statistics on your business and always have an up-to-date profit and loss statement. Learn how to read your numbers and what your benchmarks should be for each area.

Number 5: Upgrade your staff.

The most important thing you can do once you have employees is to run regular (weekly or twice weekly) training. An employee either does or does not have the aptitude to perform the role you need to be filled. They bring their motivation to the job; without it, there's not much point to them staying in this business.

Number 6: Your business should have a philosophy.

The move towards mixing philosophy with business has been a tricky one, certainly. However, it could be as simple as keeping hold of and holding yourself accountable by never abandoning the underlying development aspects of your business. Simple things like developing leadership traits and sharing positive life skills are essential.

Number 7: Focus on Retention.

The least expensive sale you ever make is the second or third sale to the same customer. Unfortunately, in most cases it's expensive, either in time or money, to attract a new customer. You may spend $500 to $1,000 or more in paid advertising to get a new customer than if you were to have a customer return. You should focus on retaining your clients as a priority.

Number 8: The Marketing Parthenon.

Relying on only one or two methods for generating new customers is not only lazy but inherently dangerous. You must develop a wide range of systems and methods for creating introductory traffic consistently. Using social media is a fantastic way to get your message and attract customers, but so are direct mail and other traditional forms of marketing.

Number 9: Separate Your Hobby from Your Business.

The majority of business owners confuse their interests as a 'hobbyist' with their role as a professional businessperson. You must not forget your interests and needs are different than the interest and needs of most of those who are interested in taking advice from you.

Number 10: Eliminate Self-Defeating Thinking and Elevate your Expectations.

Just like in the recent phenomenon 'the secret', ultimately you get what you expect and attract what you focus on intently. It's important to look for references which support your goals and objectives and to ignore the naysayers. Be very careful that you pay attention to the top 10% of the industry and ignore the opinions, pricing, and results of the rest.

I hope you will review this list. Take a blank legal pad and on the top of each page make a note of one of these points. Brainstorm with yourself about how to effectively implement each point. You're more than welcome to contact me via email with these and I will get back to you as soon as possible.

In reviewing the list, I recognize perhaps a few things are missing. I'm reading a book Don Warrener wrote and was kind enough to send me a signed limited edition of *The Kata of Business*. I haven't gotten very far, but it's got some great material in it. That being said, I doubt if I'll agree with everything, but a couple of comments in the book stuck out as especially appropriate. One was his note that the difference between a failing business owner and a successful one is 20 hours per week.

I should have made that number 11 on the list. Frankly, most business owners just don't work very hard. They show up at the office at 11 a.m. or 12 p.m. and leave at 3 or 4 p.m. and think they've done a full day. Honestly, most of the big success stories I know of start their day early and put in regular 10 to 12-hour days. They're putting in 60 to 80-hour weeks regularly. In the case of our staff, I expect them to spend daytime hours on marketing activities (9 a.m. — 5 p.m.) and evening hours focusing on client interaction, acquisition, and retention.

This quarter I'm running all my employees back through Tom Hopkin's great book, *'Master the Art of Selling'*. A key point in the book is you must "see 20 people belly-to-belly every day". January's 'millionaire skills' call included Brian Tracy giving a talk and making the same point. He said most business owners spend precious few minutes face-to-face with prospective customers in a sales effort.

If you are not talking to prospective customers (or existing ones about upgrades or referrals) then you just aren't doing what's most important for your business. You've got to have that extra 20 hours per week out there, seeing how human beings interact with your business and the products and services you provide. All the time spent on Facebook, Twitter, surfing the net, on unnecessary paperwork, or other social activity during the day just keeps you from getting out and talking to potential customers, other businesses, community leaders, and others in your community who can help your business grow.

Back to Don's book. He spends a lot of time breaking down what I have in my 10 Things list as point number three. And, he's right. Although we cover an awful lot of high-level material, it's always essential to circle back to the basics of how to answer your phone which was all covered by Toby Milroy in the A-Z day. The rule of thumb I learned from Nick Cokinos is always circling back and retrain your staff (and yourself), every 13 weeks. Always go back to basics, drill, practice, and rehearse on all the basics.

To close on this reminder of the '10 Things You Must Do to Thrive', I'll remind you to calculate your stats reports and track your numbers. It's amazing what happens when you pay attention to what's happening in all aspects of your business and how rapidly you can make huge improvements.

Beware of the Gurus

To help dispel some recently developed myths or just plain bad information, I'll give you the short version. However, at times, I will read a little like a college professor, who says, "Well, it all depends."

Cash versus billing? Here's a big: "Well, it depends."

There are state laws, especially in California, Maryland, New York, and other states and local municipalities which you must follow. First, you should make sure you are bonded or otherwise legal, depending on your local regulations. Second, if most of the revenue, on average, is routed through your monthly billing, then you will be 'leaving money on the table' and will not earn as much income as you could be. Third, if you 'push too hard' for 100% cash, then you will likely lose some customers and create a less favorable environment for your business. Fourth, if you receive cash for short term services (anything lasting between four to 12 months), then it won't make much of a positive impact on your revenue; however, if you receive cash for two, three, four or more years, then you will, on average, receive more money. Fifth, people rarely ask for refunds and you rarely need to give them (unless you have a regulatory issue which requires refunds). Taking cash payments, therefore, does not put you generally at risk of reimbursements. Sixth, how good is your business? The better your client retention, the less important it is to ask for cash early.

Finally, there are two additional *big* considerations:

Are you a good or bad money manager? You must manage your money wisely before you take large amounts of cash you haven't earned because you haven't provided the products and services to the customers yet.

How hard are you willing to work? If your billing check does not cover your monthly expenses, then you must be willing to 'make it happen' every month. Going to China, Brazil or wherever for a month will kill your business if you do not have a track record for healthy monthly revenues.

You start each month new anyway, and you must hustle every month to keep your business steady or growing.

Does Advertising Work?

I'm willing to accept the moniker of the business industry's 'marketing guru' and tell you two accurate bits of advice:

First, given the choice of a subscription to a service, for example, which didn't cost anything and one which cost $500, $750 or $1,000, in just about every case, I'll take the one for free.

Second, every business owner must put a lot of time and energy into all phases of marketing their business and should budget 12-15% of the target gross revenue on the effort. Yes, when done properly there are much more effective television, radio, direct mail and print media opportunities that work consistently.

The gurus who tell you advertising doesn't work, don't know how to make it work. A strong business, however, should be able to generate 50% or more of its leads for new customers from internal and 'grass-roots' efforts, and shouldn't have to completely rely on paid advertising for new customers.

What this argument doesn't address is the following reality of life. You should realize your marketing efforts flow through a grid which includes labor that is:

- Intensive and relatively inexpensive
- Expensive and relatively little effort required

If you have a small business especially, then you must concentrate first and foremost on the marketing methods that require effort, but relatively little money. As you grow, you will find an increasing emphasis on 'buying intros' makes more and more sense.

This explains why it is so difficult to grow your business while you are working a 'day job', with the hope of making a transition one day. In almost all cases, it just never happens because the marketing efforts require either time and money, and without both, you are left with few options or opportunities.

Are You Worried about Client Retention?

'll give you an easy and short answer. Do you want to like what you see in the mirror each day? If so, then work on excellent customer service and rapport building. Can you fix decreases in customers buying from you? No, we all have them. Harvard has a 98% graduation rate. That means 2% of those who are accepted do not complete the four-year program, which is the equivalent of a 0.04% dropout rate per month.

As an industry, we have a long way to go. While 7% may be an industry average (and it may even be 10% per month) that's not a given. I've personally seen highly successful businesses with less than a 2% rate per month. Not great by Harvard's standards, but the difference between 7% and 2% makes a phenomenal difference in your customer count, word-of-month reputation and, ultimately, your revenue.

Focus on quality service, as perceived by your customers, and all other elements of your business will take care of themselves (that is if you become an expert marketer, master of sales skills, and manage your business effectively).

Why Don't We "Walk Our Talk?"

When talking with many other entrepreneurs and business owners over the last few months, I had a 'blinding flash of the obvious'. I've always loved the reference (I borrowed it from Tom Peters).

What's the 'blinding flash of the obvious'?

All business owners say we show focus, discipline, and confidence. Many of us also claim to pass on success skills, such as goal setting, self-esteem, and self-image to other budding business owners in the making.

I see a total lack of those same attributes or a failure to translate the lessons learned physically to the operation and day-to-day running of their business. This is the number one problem of business owners.

We should all be a 'product of the product' and no, I'm not talking about a walking, talking, killing machine. What I'm talking about is becoming goal-oriented, focused on results, and having high expectations of ourselves as well as our businesses.

How Much Can You Spend to Generate More Clients?

L ast month, I presented some ideas about how much you can afford to generate more clients. Let me lead you deeper into a couple more layers of complexity of this topic.

First, to keep your average marketing budget at approximately 10% of your gross, there's one other factor to keep in mind. How many leads do you generate? How many referrals do you obtain? How many walk-ins? How many add-ons? How many are from networking events?

If you obtain half of your client base from sources such as these, then you could double how much you pay per new client and still be within your target percentage of 10% of your total gross committed to advertising.

For example (based on example #2 of last month, let's assume the business has an average lifetime customer value of $4,000-plus. The owner spent $800 on paid advertising for each customer, but half of them were from free sources. The owner would still average 10%, or $400, per enrollment — even if his/her client acquisition cost was $800 for paid advertising-generated traffic.

Second, let's compare costs at the margin with the 'average'. If you spent $5,000 a month for advertising, then the next marginal expenditure is one more dollar, or $5,001. Often in marketing, you may encounter 'declining marginal return'. In other words, for each additional dollar you spend, you receive less and less return per dollar.

A business spends $0 on marketing and advertising in any given month. For that month, it obtains five new customers as referrals and three as walk-ins. Thus, it has acquired eight new customers at $0 direct costs. If it then spends $1,000 in advertising and obtains two additional clients, then it now has two more customers at a marginal cost of $500 each. Its marginal cost per new client acquisition jumped from $0 to $500 immediately. Its average cost jumped from $0 to $200 per enrollment (10 new customers, divided by the total cost of $1,000).

How much are you willing to pay at the margin? What is the most you would be willing to pay today to receive $4,000 during the next 33 months? Ultimately, at the margin, you should be willing to pay a relatively huge amount of money for one additional client.

All the information above depends upon the lifetime value of your clients. This number includes all monies customers will pay your business, including down payments, fees, gross profit on retail items, monthly subscriptions, etc.

Use the following formula to calculate easily an approximation of this number for your business. Divide your year's gross by the number of customers acquired. For example, $500,000 gross divided by 250 new customers equals $2,000 average value per customer. If your numbers have been changing rapidly (especially if you are growing rapidly), then look at the totals of the last three years' numbers from the longer-term perspective.

You accomplish it with greater retention and cash transactions. Therefore, you increase your lifetime customer value with greater retention, retail sales, products, and services to sell to your customers.

Winners and Losers on the West Coast

It's been interesting over the last couple of weeks. We had a fabulous coaching call to kick-off March, with Toby Milroy and I extensively covering the new promotion and the A-Z of back to basics on the new client introductory process.

Next, I made quick stops in San Diego, Los Angeles, and San Francisco doing 'mini-boot camps' with members and non-members alike. If you live in California and missed these, you missed what became a very valuable small group learning opportunity; each participant left with a comprehensive marketing plan for targeting 20 or more new clients in March.

The participants represented quite a range. The most successful business represented (in San Diego) had tremendous growth out of everyone I met in the three cities. It became obvious right away in San Diego, then again in Los Angeles, I could spot the big winners from the losers, or those who have just been 'sliding along laterally' right away. No, it wasn't as if they were wearing a suit or wearing a Rolex. The evidence which gave it away was the focus. Just about everyone who attended was an accomplished entrepreneur. Many had 20, 30, or more years in operations.

The 'losers' in the group typically had two evident traits: their primary focus in conversation to other participants before the 'mini-boot camp' was predominantly on their services and how they're expanding their range of offerings to their client. They also talked about the technical aspects of their business.

In contrast, the 'winners' focused on new marketing ideas, better processes, and how to maximize their revenue per client and retention. They talked about their objectives, not from the technical side of it, but from an orientation of 'target market' success in attracting that market and their goals for growing their business.

Another sign I spotted in the 'losers', and this is most of the 'sliding along laterally' or losing 10-20% this year, was in their lack of active participation in personal education. The lowest-performing businesses had gradually stopped paying attention to the materials they were receiving, with the possibility that they let their education membership lapse. Usually, they would have stopped going to events like Quantum Leap and Extreme Success Academy. Ultimately, they had 'reverted to the familiar' and spent most of their time with peers who had similarly low expectations.

Fortunately, I believe for both groups, I have opened their eyes. Business owners who believe having 50-100 clients and charging $50 - $125 a month for their various services is doing pretty good were awakened to a much broader world with much bigger opportunities. It should be easy with all the resources I give you in all the events and coaching sessions I host, for you to run a business grossing $30,000 to $50,000 or more per month.

There are lots of examples of businesses doing very well just because they pay attention and continue to expand their education. One success example we used at the last live event was of a business that moved from $17,000 a month to well over $110,000 a month in the last 18 months. I work with them monthly on coaching calls; they've only implemented a few of the strategies I've taught them, but they do implement and have a positive belief system that it is possible.

Oh, and before I forget, the struggling businesses have another thing in common: they are surrounded by peers in the same situation. The best way to improve your results is through peer pressure to validate the potential for double, triple, or quadruple the results you are having currently. That's why there is no substitute for live events such as the Success Academy and Quantum Leap and Peer Coaching Environments. I can tell you all day long what's possible, but to see others who are no smarter than you achieving much better results is the ultimate proof you can do it yourself.

For those who think right now it's tough—we had my first business, which has been in the same location 30 years, take on 36 new customers last month. One of our newest branches had generated 79 intros from a wide variety of mostly non-paid community outreach systems. Another generated 210 intros in February from one community outreach activity.

I sincerely believe with the exclusive arrangements we've lined up with distribution companies for some new film releases this year may be a return to the absolute peak of the business industry. Add to them what should be a steadily improving economic climate and the year is going to be huge for those who keep learning, who implement what we coach them on and who get things in gear.

This month I completed an interview with Cliff Lenderman for MAIA's version of "Sounds of Success." We discussed NAPMA, MAIA, Century, and the SuperShow's ongoing excellent working relationship. A SuperShow is a great event like the old-World Conferences. Our efforts (which to date have been very successful) are to bring a smaller team of very focused business owners together to be trained extensively in 'Best Practices'. A trade show with a variety of 'Break-Out' sessions is very useful and we support those efforts. For our part, we want a 9 a.m. – midnight "roll up the sleeves and immediately go back and implement." Therefore, we have lots of stories of business owners leaving our events and jumping from $17,000 a month to over $100,000 or jumping from part-time to $200,000 a year-plus net personal income. Designed to immediately improve your income, our events are not designed for meeting the newest stars or for focusing on your technical competency but on learning the immediately implementable business and marketing practices and processes.

Growing Your Business

In my experience with coaching business owners to help them grow and develop their business, I've taken businesses from $12,000 to $17,000 a month to $35,000 to $50,000-plus. Now, how long this takes some businesses depends greatly. Some have turned around their business in as little as 90 days; others took 9 to 15 months. Either way, the hidden truth of most of these quick turnarounds was the need to 'deprogram' them of convoluted systems and processes as well as simplify their operation. Many suffered the delusion that the way to success was to keep laying on additional processes and new services, subscriptions and products. Let me tell you now — it isn't.

This leads me to my next topic. A few months ago, I was talking to one of my early colleagues I had advised and coached, one who had been a participant in the first marketing boot camp. At the time, he had a $7,000 a month business and has transformed his business revenue into $1,000,000-plus a month. He also has several other multi-million-dollar businesses, so it's safe to say he was doing amazingly well. So, as we were talking and 'catching up', he reminded me of several pieces of advice I gave him when we first met.

The first, however blunt and brutal, was:

"Any brain-dead idiot can run a $20,000-plus per month business."

With hindsight, fortunately or otherwise, I might say this in a more polite way. However, that sentiment is truer now than ever. In the late 1970s and early 1980s, a brand had nine branches of their business, then 12 businesses averaging more than that amount 30 years ago. For many years, as early as 1983, my businesses which were employee-owned all averaged more than that number. I remember one year (1991 I believe) was $1,680,000, with five businesses all absentee owner-employee operated. To do the math for you, that's an average of $28,000 a month across five locations for the year. That was not an unusual year.

There are lots of business owners doing way less than that number. My question is, "Why?" I'm convinced there are several main reasons.

Many businesses have inappropriately low expectations. There were some I met in California who legitimately didn't know t it was possible to net $100,000 or more by running a single branch of their business. Once your eyes are opened and you believe it is possible, then more opportunities will open up for you.

Over the years, I have found many business owners have a lack of personal education; they believe their years of study in a business qualification entitles them to success, without continuing to learn on top of that. The unfortunate reality for them is success in running a business is more dependent on knowledge of marketing, sales, and service than it is on technical mastery. You need to be aware of many more skills and areas which will help your business to thrive. If you don't learn about marketing, for example, how do you expect anyone to know about what you can offer them?

There's something special about the people I have taught about business. One of them, for example, has been the general manager of a multi-million-dollar chain, and now runs a multi-million-dollar business chain, with individual branches grossing as much as $750,000 a year. He's learned to move from working as part of a business to management, and then to the business owner over the years. And, by god, he's earned it. He has the drive and determination to push forward and achieve his goals, no matter what they are. He took extra courses to develop himself; he devoted most evenings and weekends to develop his business. So, the question to you is: are you willing to put in the same 'pain and suffering' on educating yourself as a business owner?

Unfortunately, there is an abundance of 'false gurus' everywhere. There are so many of those running around the business industry giving advice and they haven't truly been successfully running a business themselves. For some of them, the last time they actively ran a business was many, many years ago. It goes without saying in this context, the environment in the business community has dramatically changed in that time and won't be the same now as it was back then. Some owners run personality-based businesses with some success, and then try to teach their methods to you; this might not be something you want to do.

I was having a conversation with several associates recently about this phenomenon. The comment was that I was responsible for most of the guys running around right now who fit the above description. I think a more appropriate, although simplistic, the observation was more recently, as I started coaching and offering exclusive boot camps, a series of former clients had some success from my teaching (i.e. $12,000 to $30,000 in a few months), then made the unfortunate conclusion they had 'arrived'. They then started running around sharing their "wisdom" with the industry.

Do you know the quote below?

"A winner knows how much he still has to learn, even when considered an expert by others.

A loser wants to be considered an expert by others before he has learned enough to know how little he knows."

— Sydney Harris

It's unfortunate for many in the industry who don't know the people who are real and trying to give good advice, from who's not real and are just trying to make money because they think they know best. Here are a few questions for you to ask a potential guru, to see if they are genuine:

- Where did this 'guru' gain their knowledge; and do they openly and freely acknowledge their debt of gratitude?
- Do they currently operate successful businesses? (I say businesses, rather than business, since many people who run a successful single branch of their business are relying on their own 'force of personality' more so than a system that works. If they were to open a second branch, then it probably would fail due to their bad system and processes.) If not, how long has it been and what was their track record then?
- Is their advice enough to take you to the highest levels of the industry; or are they limited in their own 'scope and capability'?
- How's their ROI (return on investment)? I've always promised high-end coaching clients a minimum of a 10-to- return on investment. In most cases, they've received 20-to-1 or more return on any money they've invested with me — and this is something I can certainly prove.

I've recently seen a high-profile long-time guru in the industry, directly and indirectly, bashing me. He doesn't explain he learned how to run a business mostly from me and Jeff Smith. He doesn't explain he never ran a particularly successful business and he, frankly, didn't enjoy it much when he did. He doesn't explain his advice is mostly tailored to "be what independent business owners want to hear" not what they need to hear to truly be successful. And finally, he doesn't explain he's so distanced from running businesses and the day-to-day operations of running a business that he's completely in the dark as to what's working today in the current market and environment.

There are several 'gurus' coaching a "run to be a successful business" without truly understanding the business market to begin with, let alone the niche your business will be in. Is there a market for your business? You bet. Is it the right market for many or most businesses, if they have some knowledge in their niche? No. Make sure you take advice from someone who understands the real forces at work in your specific industry.

And, to get back to point one: I freely acknowledge my "Debt of Gratitude" to teachers and mentors I have had in the past. There are so many — too many to mention at this point.

Crisis Hits

When I say, crisis hits, I am not talking about hurricanes, earthquakes or any other recent natural disasters. I am referring to a recent and dangerous trend in the business industry that is not only risky for individual businesses but also, I'm afraid I may just reawaken the staff of state Attorneys' General offices around the U.S. (and their equivalent elsewhere).

What's that trend? Recently, several industry 'gurus' focused on cash programs as the ultimate solution for business operations. This overwhelming emphasis on cash threatens to wreak havoc on the industry, especially when it is combined with arguably 'hard-core' sales tactics and often, disreputable or, at the very least, apathetic approaches to long-term customer service.

Please review with me the first example of the problem. I have spoken with many business owners recently as I have mentioned previously; some of them have aggressively adopted what I will characterize as the following:

- Aggressive sales efforts focused on 'cashing out' 100% of their existing clients.
- Aggressive sales strategies to 'cash-out' 100% of subscriptions and services.
- Disdain for fee billing and billing companies.
- Inadequate and/or heavily 'labor-intensive' marketing efforts with limited 'leverage'.

Often, these strategies are combined with a 'what the hell' attitude regarding customer service. These business owners have also adopted the viewpoint that they will inevitably lose their clients anyway; they're not able to stop losing the client, so why try and retain them?

Adopting all or several of these methods and attitudes often results in the following scenario: a business owner learns these new tools, implements them suddenly and asks for cash payments from all of his clients.

It's easy to predict what inevitably happens: the business owner doubles, sometimes, even triples his best month ever — nothing wrong with that as far as it goes. What happens next really wreaks havoc. Without a very strong and effective marketing program, a business that has cashed out all its clients without big numbers, ultimately experiences serious trouble.

I've seen a business owner who learned all these new systems; they then cashed out every customer in his database and hit the malls with a clipboard and a serious head of steam for two or three months. Thrilled with his huge cash flow, the business owner buys a Corvette or a Porsche and a Rolex or two, spending all the money on rapidly depreciating assets, such as jewelry, cars, vacations, high-priced restaurants, or even in the best case, his own 'McMansion', which locks him into a big payment, creating an asset that is not liquid. In straightforward terms, he has blown the money quickly and completely. What happens next? Inevitably, his record cash results cannot be maintained, and the monthly bottom line becomes just average months with 20%, 50%, and even 75% less revenue than previously.

'Mr. Cash-Out', the business owner who has foolishly spent all the money, awakes one morning to realize a couple of horrible truths.

- He has pissed off X number of clients and many no longer use his services, so his client base has decreased at an alarming rate.
- He is cash-poor with a severely reduced cash flow and is on the brink of insolvency.

There are thoughts concerning cash-outs, and each has its rabid rank of supporters. Frankly, I don't endorse either.

Thought #1: Ask for cash. If your clients pay you in full, then you have 100% of their money.

Thought #2: It's illegal, unethical and immoral to take the cash, so process your client's payments through a billing system.

Frankly, I like big cash deals. What I don't like is seeing business owners take hundreds of thousands of dollars in cash, and then through financial mismanagement or miscalculation, they are forced to close their businesses, which is an invitation for regulatory scrutiny.

Nick Cokinos, the founder of Educational Funding Company, has preached the correct strategy for years, which is utilizing a contingent-liability fund. Quite simply, you deposit all money for the services you haven't provided for the client yet into savings accounts — liquid interest-bearing investments. You don't withdraw the money until you've earned it, and the client has received their product or service. For example, a business owner accepts a three-year subscription paid-in-full. He deposits one-sixth of the cash-out in his checking account as current income; however, he should deposit only 1/36th this month. Every month, he withdraws an amount equal to the services provided during that month (or would be provided if the client cancels) and deposits the amount in his checking account as earned income.

The alternative approach is just as valid. Build your billing check to cover all your monthly expenses. When you take cash programs, invest the money personally to build wealth. Create your lifestyle as your business and your wealth will grow — not from short-term bursts, but long-term investing.

Are You Ready to Commit to Success?

'm convinced this year is going to be a great year for the business industry. More specifically for you, the fact you are reading this means you are going to implement (more about this later) and grow.

It's certainly true the last 24 months, between the recession in general and the credit crisis, have been rough on all small businesses. In some areas, unemployment skyrocketed, and there was a general 'malaise' among consumers.

The economy is creeping back. It's not roaring back yet, but it is well on the way. Employment lags (not leads) the economic recovery and while the housing market may not reach the previous 'bubble highs', it's clear all around us that the economy is rebounding.

In retrospect, I'm sure it bottomed out and began rebounding long before President Obama tinkered with anything or accelerated government overspending — however that's a topic for another time. The current reality is consumer spending is back up; even the car companies are starting to show a profit again. My favorite, Apple, had their best first quarter ever, and their best quarter, excluding Christmas season, ever. And that was before the iPad sold 500,000 units in a week. Even Martha Stewart on Fox Business was bragging about their sales and profits being way up in all channels, including at Macy's. How's this year look? Well, it depends on your industry, and if there is anything topical which will relate to your industry.

Maybe you should see what films, books, plays or TV shows are coming out, to see if they do link back to your products and services. If they are (and they're not distant or tentative links) then it is useful to incorporate them into your social media marketing plan. If done properly, not only will it increase your engagement, but it will create an exciting atmosphere for your staff and yourself as well.

Truthfully, it's events and opportunities like these that can help bring in a large flow of customers. I've always worked to have a good excuse for huge influxes at least a couple of times per year. I've looked for at least a quarterly reason to drive customer acquisition. Maybe it's just me, but a key element of sales management always seems to be a good excuse for peak results and something different to gain attention and focus on results.

What will guarantee your success? I hate to keep banging the same drum, but go back and read the 10 things you must do to be successful. They include research your pricing and charge accordingly for your customers, fix your sales ratios, offer continually better service to your customers from their perspective, and market, market, market to add 20-plus new customers per month.

The difference is implementation. I am continually amazed and flabbergasted by the number of people who pay lip service to a desire to be successful...who then do little or nothing. I'm going to share with you today my two favorite quotes. Each of which occupied page one or two of my day-planner for years. Both have to do with truly accomplishing things rather than learning, hoping, planning, expecting, or otherwise preparing for, rather than achieving successful outcomes.

The first favorite quote is:

"Winners remember results, losers remember reasons."

That's a very important one to anchor in for yourself. I repeatedly talk to business owners who share with me all the reasons why what I'm suggesting won't work in their town, their city, for their target demographic, or with their style. They create a long list of reasons for everything that could go wrong, might go wrong, should go wrong. If they put 1/10th of that energy into just going and doing it, they might accomplish something.

The next thing these same people do, when asked about their stats or their past results, is to give me the long list of reasons of how they did everything right and things magically didn't work out. The excuse du jour is 'the economy'. Everyone's unemployed, has no money, isn't willing to pay for, and it goes on and on. It's interesting that at the same time, 500,000-plus 'early adopters' paid $500 and more for an iPad without knowing what they were going to use it for or even really what it would do.

Now, don't miss the point. If you are in downtown Detroit with a 40% vacancy and 35% unemployment — then you may be right. The question is why isn't your U-Haul packed and headed to areas with more opportunity?

The second quote is all about commitment. Are you truly committed to being successful as a business owner? I've got to remind you the 'wait and see' method always leads to failure. You must be an active and committed participant in your success. Unless you set a real goal and publicly commit yourself to be in the top 20% of your industry, you are doomed to mediocrity and frankly to struggling financially.

The quote is this:

"Until one is committed, there is hesitancy, the chance to draw back, and always ineffectiveness."

Concerning all acts of initiative and creation, there is one elementary truth the ignorance of which kills countless ideas and splendid plans which is the moment one commits oneself, then providence moves too.

All sorts of things occur to help one which would never otherwise have occurred. A whole stream of events issues from the decision, raising in one's favor all manner of unforeseen incidents, meetings and material assistance which no man could have dreamed would have come his way. I have learned a deep respect for one of Goethe's couplets:

'Whatever you can do, or dream you can, begin it! Boldness has genius, magic, and power in it.'

— W.H. Murray, of the Scottish Himalayan Expedition

My group in California didn't have the benefits of coaching or events to help boost their business. These $7,000—$12,000 businesses were happy with their results, not realizing others "not as smart as them" in no better locations were netting more than they were grossing. And still others were running $35,000—$100,000 a month business with their same style and similar clientele. The belief in what's possible is extremely valuable. It's why you've got to surround yourself with people who are doing better than yourself. This is so you can always aim high and strive to be the best in your area and your industry.

A similar example would be when I engaged in an industry discussion board recently about operations within the business. A business operator in my home state of Oklahoma chipped in and bragged about running a very successful operation which was doing $15,000 a month. I guess 'very successful' depends upon your perspective. While in Atlanta I spoke with two different business owners who were grossing over $100,000 a month (one from Miami, the other from Nashville or Memphis). One business was technically open seven days a week, 24 hours a day. While in San Antonio, we visited another location with over 3,000 members.

The $15,000 a month business thought they were setting the world on fire. Since they don't attend any of my events or read my materials, they are not reading this now and are probably only interacting with other business owners who are, to quote Tom Hopkins: "more screwed up than they are." They don't understand the six-figure income potential of their business. It's the same type of owner who only wants free advice and won't invest to learn from those who have been there, done that in the industry. Their loss, your gain.

Manage Your Time, Live Your Life

In business operations, there are two major time-management problems business owners encounter.

First: Deciding their workday is from 9 a.m. to 5 p.m., then spending their day with a variety of time-wasting activities. Many important activities should be accomplished during non-prime time hours.

Remember during working hours if you are not personally interacting with your employees and your customers, then you are misusing your time. These are typically the only hours when you can communicate with your customers, so you should be. What should you do during non-working hours? External promotional and marketing activities such as:

- Meeting with local businesses and attending network events.
- Meeting with local merchants to develop co-promotional opportunities.
- Researching advertising and marketing opportunities.
- Writing marketing letters to your old prospects.
- Reviewing your list of customers and former customers, seeing if you can upsell them or get them to re-join you.
- Updating your computer system and keeping your stats up to date.

The main issue is to distinguish between prime-time activities and non-prime time activities. All administrative duties should be accomplished only during non-prime time hours.

Second: Failing to manage time effectively on an hour-by-hour and minute-by-minute basis.

How do you manage your time effectively? Use an effective planning system is my recommendation. I prefer Franklin Planners. They are more expensive than some of the other systems, but, given the value of this system to your life and your business, it is well worth the expense. When using the Franklin system, I plan many activities quarterly and monthly — instead of focusing on every quarter-hour. If you keep your objectives clear, then it can be relatively easy to manage your evening hours.

Use an adequate management software system to keep your appointments and prospects' stats under control. Currently, there are several fine systems on the market.

Prioritize appropriately. I highly recommend you read First Things First by Steven Covey, or, at least, study the chapter 7 Habits of Highly Effective People.

To summarize Covey's concepts, all activities fall into one of four quadrants:

- Urgent and Important.
- Not Urgent and Important.
- Urgent and Not Important.
- Not Urgent and Not Important.

A business during prime-time hours (9 a.m. to 5 p.m.) is full of constant customer queries, emails, phone calls, and this is on a minute-by-minute basis. For your evening to be effective, remember there are only three important elements: attracting customers, retention, and renewals. If an activity does not positively contribute to one of these elements, then it falls into the "Not Important" category.

Mediocre business owners fail to focus on those important areas, that are not urgent. Generally important, but not urgent areas include:

- Internal and external marketing efforts.
- Client retention.
- Renewal preparation (if you have subscriptions).
- A note about clients and your time: with few exceptions, clients, of one or two types, can consume your time. Your model customers who are loyalists and your negative and disgruntled clients who are full of complaints. You must be careful not to devote too much prime time to clients in either of these categories, but instead, find a balance between the two.

Your model customers will spend time talking, and investing time in your presence, because they love the services and products available to them, the ones you provide. Your negative clients often have a negative outlook on their lives, and just want to complain to anyone who will listen. In any conversation of this type, work on keeping the conversation short and on the subject it should be.

A few ways to accomplish this is don't sit down, don't go in your office — address the issues at hand quickly and directly, suggest scheduling a specific appointment time when it's appropriate for your schedule. The third is by not spending excess time on hobby activities while rationalizing you are working on your business, and the fourth is failing to structure your day effectively. To get the most out of your day, it's important to determine how you function best, and then plan your activities during your peak times of efficiency.

A few years ago, there seemed to be this myth that successful entrepreneurs and business owners rose at dawn and were in their office by 8:00 am. This works quite well for some of my closest friends, but, for me, this has always been massively counter-productive.

A lot of business owners are at their absolute peak between the hours of 10 a.m. and 12 p.m. You must determine which of your creative hours are for planning and development, and structure your days to hit your peak during prime-time hours. Even if you're not at your peak between 10 am and midday, as long as you can identify where your prime hours are and utilize them.

For myself, I am most creative late at night. When most of my friends are climbing into bed, I am just starting work. What you're reading right now was probably written between 11 p.m. and 3 a.m. I like to start my day mid-morning, take a break mid-day, and then hit the operations side of the business hard during my prime time.

Depending upon what I need to accomplish, I will either take a break and go to a movie, grab a quick bite to eat, and then work on my creative projects — either writing lesson plans, designing ad campaigns and writing.

For best time management, you can do much more work when no one is around to interrupt and the phones aren't ringing. If you are an early bird, then 5 a.m. or 6 a.m. might be best for you. Again, for me, my creative tasks are accomplished after 11 p.m. If I return your e-mail, then it may be at 2 or 3 a.m.

"Positioning" Your Business

Years ago, I read an interesting book called *Positioning: The Battle for Your Mind*. Some of the concepts presented a conflict with the general direct-response position I hold and propose throughout this column; however, a couple of concepts are worth revisiting.

What Are You Promoting?

The example used in the book (keep in mind this book was first published years ago) was about IBM's introduction of the personal computer (PC). You may be old enough to remember when IBM introduced its first PC, several different makers were pushing various systems. Apple had already made a splash with the Macintosh computer; the Osborn computer was big; Kaypro, Tandy, Commodore, and others already had systems available with competing for operating systems and structures. The industry was fragmented with no standards.

IBM could have introduced its new product by positioning it against its direct competitors — for example, why its product is better than Apple's or Tandy's. However, IBM did not choose that approach. Its management realized, quite appropriately, that battling over the very small number of hobbyists who already owned or were ready to buy a microcomputer was futile.

Instead, IBM took the tact of promoting why everyone should have a PC. IBM created a non-threatening mascot of sorts (the Tramp of Charlie Chaplain fame) and began a series of ads which explained the value of a PC in the home or office — always without reference to their direct competitors or other manufacturers. IBM's logic was if it promoted the virtues of these machines, then IBM would gradually be recognized as the leader in the industry and it would expand the number of people using computers rather than battle for market share.

I think this would be a very lousy approach for beer-makers or soft-drink manufacturers who are battling for market share in declining overall markets; however, for the majority of other businesses, this is generally a great approach.

What Is Memorable about Your Business?

If you plan to advertise and promote your business repetitively for many years, then you should be concerned about several details. Your ads should have a consistent look and feel so they become recognizable and memorable. There should always be some consistent pieces of content — may be the format of your business name or logo and perhaps, a common tag line. Your ads should have a consistent appeal to a specific audience. If you try to be everything for everyone, then you'll be nothing to no one! I'd rather be consistent with a target audience and become known for that niche than being spread across the board.

Your business should have an easy-to-remember name. Some businesses use names that are quite complicated, unpronounceable by the general public, and all-round difficult to remember. These businesses soon realize this isn't the way to go. It is strongly recommended to choose a name that will be easy to remember and pronounce.

Now is the Time to Hustle Like Never Before

I sincerely believe we are at a marvelous 'inflection point' in the business industry. I've seen this twice before. First in 1985, second in 1991. We combine two things right now which make the next 18 months considerably different than the last 18 months.

First, is the economic recovery. Since the run-up to the presidential election, generally, we've been in one of the worst recessions in this century. That makes it difficult for all businesses, especially those who rely on "discretionary spending" to get rolling.

The economy isn't fully back, but consumer optimism is up and overall consumer spending is coming back. Some areas such as real estate and employment are 'lagging, not leading' indicators, and it will be a long while until real estate returns to 'bubble highs' (if ever, in inflation-adjusted terms). However, the economy is recovering, and consumers are starting to spend again.

Second, you can't sit on the sidelines. You must be spending on direct mail (mail multiple 'Grabber Mailings' to your prospect database), you must be at networking events, business fairs and business expos (target 2,000—3,000 leads from these this summer), and theaters. You must be on TV and in newspaper inserts.

These are all things I did in 1985, 1986, 1987 with huge results. However, I believe many (not all) of our businesses will be at 500 active and $100,000-plus-plus-plus revenue by early or mid-fall.

Let me take a deep breath and recognize a couple of things that may not be obvious.

A bunch of business owners are running around adding new programs and products thinking that as traditional stylists they must follow this trend to stay afloat. Often times they rush to add new things without asking if there is an overwhelming demand for the program. Don't get me wrong — I do believe there is a market for quality programs in every business industry. However, I think it's a huge mistake to layer contradictory programs onto your business or adapt a current service "because everyone else is doing it," rather than focusing on a market and pursuing it effectively.

It's difficult, if not impossible, to be "all things to all people". Think of any brand that comes to mind. I'll throw a couple of examples. What's BMW? "The Ultimate Driving Machine", i.e. sporty, responsive cars that are fun to drive. What's Apple? Quality, easy to use stuff. Certainly not the cheapest (I read they have a 75% plus market penetration of laptops priced at $1,000 and up). Pick any other strong brand and see if they are trying to be all things to all people. What should you do? Pick a market in which you are competent and excited about servicing and focus all your efforts on that market.

How To "Turbo Charge" Your Results

The key components are simple: know what you want to accomplish, learn the necessary skills, then execute your plan. It's amazing to me how many people sit on their butt, do nothing and then complain about how hard they are working. Take action, be busy, make it happen!

What is the next step? I hate to be a broken record on some subjects, but you must increase your prices, and to do so, certain factors must be in place. For example: after reviewing the revenues of one of my coaching clients recently, I calculated if he would just increase his down payment, then he'd add $98,000 in revenue with the same number of clients. Guess what happened? I spent three months banging on my drum before he did anything. He added $0 in revenue. After a while, he decided to listen and finally "took the plunge." Guess what happened?

His client ratios increased — yes, at a higher price point, he obtained more clients. His staff (he has multiple branches in different locations) told him my strategy made things much easier. As they say in direct-response TV commercials – "but wait, there's more!"

Before you think he is an isolated example, please let me explain I often find this to be the case; the only limitation is in the minds of the owner, program director or whoever is running the business, not in the minds of prospective clients.

What should *you* charge? It depends on multiple factors. What's the most important factor? That would be creating a perception of value. You must present your program, product or service as being valuable — *very* valuable. Once you've established the value, then it's only a matter of what I refer to as "fishing in the right pond", i.e. marketing to your target demographic who can afford your prices.

As we are covering such a broad range of industries and areas of business, I can't provide a blanket price recommendation, but when it comes to pricing, there are many reasons and excuses I hear for not charging as much as people think. These are:

"I can't charge that much because my competition charges $X." and *"My clients cannot afford that much."*

Frankly, my concern about your competition is exactly zip, zilch, and nada. Who cares what they are charging? If your prospects are making price comparisons, then it is due to one of two problems: either you are not very impressive during their first impression of you or you are failing to 'market in a vacuum'. These could mean all sorts of things, especially with the first impressions: this could be your website, your presentation, the building, your social media presence — anything you showcase to the public.

The 'market in a vacuum' concept is one I have addressed before. Essentially, it is what occurs when you rely on the Yellow Pages or other similar marketing resources for most of your clients. They will be prone to make price comparisons. If you are following my advice, however, then you won't experience this problem.

The other concern is typically a figment of your imagination: "They can't afford it?" Take a minute to observe and understand the spending habits of your clients. Maybe you are in a poverty-stricken area, in which case it's recommended you should move. Otherwise, I'll bet your clients (and prospective clients) are spending much bigger sums on many other purchases than what I suggest you charge.

For example, a family recently explained they couldn't afford their renewal since they had spent $12,000 on a Disney World vacation! A couple of weeks with the Mouse and $12,000 were gone!

So, just a bit of caution about your current clients. You should keep in mind your current clients have already been very solidly sold on what you are worth. You have 'pre-framed' them to think of your services, no matter how much they love them, to be worth what you've asked them to pay.

It's difficult (not impossible, but difficult) to increase the price they pay to receive the same training they are currently receiving. There is a strategy which will allow you to increase your prices as well, but I won't go into it now. We've made those increases at my business a few times in the past and have experienced amazingly huge financial results.

Who Is Our Competition?

I've addressed how shortsighted it is to focus on other businesses that provide similar services as your competition. To help further your understanding, let me share with you several real-world observations.

Price is irrelevant in comparison to what other businesses charge. Starting in 1983, I moved into Denver and grew from zero to 1,500 clients during a little more than 18 months, while charging between 50% and 100% more than the average of other businesses.

How was I able to do that? There are many factors, but some of them are:

1. Predominantly 'marketing in a vacuum', i.e. creating the market for your services and drawing them to me, rather than actively competing for individuals seeking those particular services. Few of those clients came from the Yellow Pages, the sign on the building or more traditional marketing methods. Almost all of them were generated by aggressively pursuing 'suspects' who fit our profile (the target demographic, essentially) and convincing them what we provided was valuable and worth their time.

2. An early recognition few prospects (or active clients, for that matter) actively shop price. Many people who call the business or walk in the door asking about price; however, anyone even marginally skilled in telephone sales skills quickly makes price a non-issue.

3. A clear understanding price is only important to most people concerning 'value'. With any service like ours, the prospect has difficulty equating value to what he or she is receiving. With a tangible product, customers are more likely to try to compute an expectation of the cost of materials and the difficulty of manufacture.

They're only able to assess the value of your training is your presentation of your program, your facility, and most importantly, your staff and you. They will judge value mostly on whether they like, respect and trust the people they meet.

Next, they will judge value, according to the benefits of your program and the amount of 'social proof' you provide to increase their believability of that outcome for them.

"Price determines the perception of quality." As counter-intuitive as this may be, prospects do shop for certain types of businesses will often choose the more expensive — knowing nothing else. The reason is whichever business is the most expensive must be the best and, frankly, most of us want the best products and services we can afford, not the cheapest. Granted, there may be exceptions to that statement, however, just because you shop at Wal-Mart or Sam's Club doesn't mean you don't want the best. It just means you want the lowest price on a quality branded product.

Consumers have been taught the 'knee-jerk' reaction, attributing price and known brands with quality — and 'inexpensive' to being 'cheap'. Quick: which do you emotionally want, a Porsche or Subaru sports car? How about a Rolex or Timex? The Timex or Subaru may have all the features you want and maybe better.

In my case, I have several expensive watches, but my 25-year-old Seiko with a battery keeps much better time. I have a $19 wall clock which keeps much better time than the Rolexes or the Breitling. I drive a 911 Twin Turbo but could have bought a Subaru with a nearly comparable performance for much less than half the cost. For example, for our household, we often purchase branded food items from Sam's, but not the cheapest generic or 'unknown' products. A service is essentially selling the unknown. Consumers are unable to judge quality systematically; they're only able to judge based upon the factors in Item 3 above.

In reality, your mission should be to show the incredible benefits of what you can provide your customers — your products, services, etc.

Big Winners, Winners, and the Mediocre Majority

In extensive conversations I had with Toby Milroy and Jeff Smith, we reviewed results I had from several years working with coaching clients. It's interesting to review the results of these past experiences and extrapolate them into how to help members in the future develop their businesses.

Results from coaching clients tend to be in one of two groups:

- The starting point of $12,000 a month or less. Typically, they would argue implementation (it won't work in my town, city, with my style, with my staff, with my clients) or they would change things to the point of being unrecognizable, then do nothing until their credit card maxed and they bailed out.

- Starting point of $13,000 to $20,000 a month. Typically, they would get to $30,000 to $50,000 quickly. The quickest would be 90 days: it was typically more towards 7–10 months for a lot.

These results were accomplished from one coaching group teleconference a month. The Millionaire Skills Call monthly is a coaching members' private website and discussion board and a 30-minute one-on-one monthly call. Coaching members were also invited to a live event twice a year for a day or two. They were typically receiving a fax a few times per month about current priorities as well.

First, let's talk about those who failed in the process. The failures in any business tend to share commonalities. Let's start with a couple of universal realities. The world generally is divided into 5% big winners, 15% winners and 80% in the mediocre (or worse) majority. These numbers will vary, depending on the industry. Knowing industry as I do, I think the 5% and 15% ratios are generous for the business industry. There's a relatively small number of business owners who are investing large sums of money and time in themselves and their businesses to make massive improvements. Most business owners in general, spend little or no time or money to improve their business or financial results.

What are the commonalities of the losers? The first and most common is for 80% or more, much of the 15% spend the bulk of the time and money they do spend on personal and professional improvement on technical skills. They fly to Brazil or China to train in their chosen field. They spend 10, 15, 20 or more hours per week on their training and on perfecting their skills. Don't get me wrong: your technical knowledge is important. However, low-performing businesses can't see beyond technical knowledge to the skills truly necessary for their professional growth.

Second, which is common at least among the 80% who achieve little or nothing, is the tendency to discount professional skills and systems with erroneous excuses. They say things like "... that's in a big city, it wouldn't work in my area. That's East Coast, it won't work in the Midwest." You get the idea. They say it won't work with my clients, in my area, with my style, with my staff and then they do nothing.

Third, they want everything for free. Look at the free internet discussion boards and Facebook groups. Many of the participants are looking for free advice and are unwilling to pay for quality training. It's trite but true — you get what you pay for. In the Internet world, there's an often-misquoted line: "information wants to be free." The concept has led to many failed business ventures and ultimately is a foundation for an ongoing media battle which is costing big media companies billions of dollars. You've seen Steve Jobs and many others chip in on this conversation the problem online is that free information is most often worth exactly that...nothing. In a world of bloggers, how do you sort fact from fiction, the value from rubbish?

The exact quote, by the way, was by Stewart Brand:

"In fall 1984, at the first Hackers' Conference, I said in one discussion session: 'On the one hand information wants to be expensive because it's so valuable. The right information in the right place just changes your life. On the other hand, information wants to be free, because the cost of getting it out is getting lower and lower all the time. So, you have these two fighting against each other'."

Those who are unwilling to invest in their education and in tools and systems to grow their business will be left to complain on the sidelines about all those who were willing to invest in their growth and development.

Fourth, most people fail to achieve much because they have a belief system about what they can achieve. They limit themselves to that level. No matter how often they see others running $500,000 or $1,000,000 a year business, they get stuck at $100,000 a year and can never rise above it because they believe they've internalized and never changed.

Frankly, some of the biggest leaps I've made in my career was when I was introduced to a new speaker or consultant through a live event, during their 45-minute or 1-hour presentation then was offered an opportunity to study the topic more in-depth. One which leaps to mind was Jonathan Mizel (an 'internet marketing guru') who sold me a box of materials containing probably 30 hours of training, following a 45-minute presentation I was incredibly impressed with, then membership in his newsletter. I managed to meet him for lunch later but took special care to read the entire archives of his newsletter website (two three-ring notebooks full of written material) so I'd be prepared to ask intelligent questions.

Frankly, if someone listens to me or anyone else for an hour or two, they've been introduced to a topic but they are far from mastery. Imagine a marketing trainee attending a two-hour seminar on marketing campaigns and they walk out thinking they'd learned the topic.

One of the best direct response marketing books you should read was written in 1923 by a gentleman by the name of Claude Hopkins. It's called Scientific Advertising. Another one, Ogilvy on Advertising, was written in 1985. Some of the major concepts you should be using in your business were first articulated in 1923 and before then. However, if you have not read those books and the many others on the topic and applied them to your business through extensive testing and experimentation, then the concepts are new — to you. And frankly, to 99% of business owners as well.

At the other extreme, new things are happening in many areas. An easy example is with internet marketing, which is changing every month, as there are *lots* of new things happening you should know about, which are useful to your business.

Honestly, one of the biggest impediments to business owners is believing the methods of running your business of 10, 20 or even 100 years ago were as good as it gets. In that area, learning and adding modern methodology is essential to your growth, and is not available from anyone who's not currently working directly with hundreds or thousands of clients. It's important to combine modern educational technology with the constantly updated structure to maximize both your client retention and the quality of you and your employee's skills.

Another past guru in the industry ranted and raved recently about there being no 'secrets' in the industry, noting we'd promised to reveal the 'secrets to success' at an upcoming event. I heard one described recently to me by an expert this way: "It may not be a 'secret' to you...but if the client does not know it or understand it, then it's certainly a 'secret' to them."

Are there secrets to success? There are certain things the top 1% of the business industry know and apply that the other 99% haven't been taught or haven't applied properly. There are certainly "subtle distinctions" which are the difference between mediocrity and success. In a book I'm reading right now, David Ogilvy described how he experienced 19 times the improvement in an advertisement from one change — that's 1900% improvement.

That having been said, how do you value advice? This one is difficult to answer. I like to look at it as a return on investment. I've seen free bad advice, which ended up costing those business owners many thousands of dollars as a result. Some 'lesser gurus cost business owners $100,000 or more in lost opportunities and lost clients just last summer with bad advice about how to utilize films as part of their marketing strategy.

With my coaching clients, I've always promised a "10x return on investment", or in other words, for every $1,000 they spend, they could expect $10,000 back — if, and only if they applied what I taught them. Anyway, the typical free advice you get from Internet sites and the guys who charge you up to $100 a month for a 'bunch of stuff' is costing you thousands of dollars in lost revenue. In our case, we have many years of real-world experience at the table teaching you how to be a true professional, how to run your business successfully, and how to earn a solid six-figure income along the way.

Oh, and back to point number two. Those coaching clients who went from $15,000 to $30,000 in 90 days or nine months, and those who went to $50,000 or more — what were their commonalities? Mostly they *implemented*. I cannot stress this enough. They took direction on faith and just went and immediately got going. They didn't look for reasons why it wouldn't work; they didn't let their employees get in the way; they took the ideas and immediately ran with them.

Some of the specific implementation processes I gave everyone who got to $50,000 a month or more was as follows:

- Keep good statistics (for a monthly review with me).
- Fix pricing (raise their prices).
- Have different levels of service - upgrades (50% to 100%).
- Review and fix (if necessary) the initial process to get the clients on board.
- Look at initial pricing and products.
- "Open the floodgates" to the introductory process.
- Along the way, these coaching clients learned more sophisticated marketing and advertising theory as well as good strategies and applied them to their own business.
- Suggested reading for you:
- *Tested Advertising Methods;* Caples.
- *Ogilvy on Advertising*; Ogilvy.
- *My Life in Advertising* and *Scientific Advertising*; Hopkins.

A Great Experience

An interesting and very important topic called 'abundance mentality' was addressed at a recent business event. That was why I hired Lee Milteer, a professional speaker, and trainer, to work with my staff, franchise business owners and personal coaching clients, and provide you with exclusive information on the subject of the 'millionaire mindset'.

It's just amazing how many business owners think of money and other resources as being limited rather than infinite. In general, small businesses, as well as bigger businesses seem to suffer from several major hang-ups about money.

First, they think it is wrong to make money by providing the services they do. To me, that's silly. It's no more inappropriate than a singer being paid for concerts and albums, a racecar driver being paid for a driving career, or a writer being paid to write articles and blogs. These are all good examples of services which have every right to be paid for. It's all about knowing your worth and believing what you do makes a difference to others — because it does.

Second, some business owners think there comes a point where their clients are paying more than they should be paying. They've made three erroneous assumptions:

1) Charging what clients are willing to pay might be charging too much.

2) Charging more than other business owners are willing to charge for a similar service is inappropriate.

3) Excluding some clients who are unable to pay is somehow inappropriate.

Third, business owners think being "in it for the money" is somehow at odds with being the best businessman and employer — another strange and erroneous concept.

You must convince yourself there is as much money and other resources available as you expect, need and request. Finances are not limited. We live in an affluent society, and there's no reason why you shouldn't receive a share of that affluence.

Do me a quick favor and count how much cash you have in your wallet, money clip or wrapped around your credit cards with a rubber band. Go ahead, I'll wait.

I'm willing to bet you have less than $500, most likely, less than $100. I have $2,132 in cash in my wallet (you know the green paper money they still make). Let me ask you a few questions: If you have $32 in your wallet and I have $2,132 in mine, then who do you think will recognize an opportunity faster? Who do you think will think in terms of "there's plenty" first? Who do you think will panic quicker when the next little crisis hits? If you want your business to be financially viable, then consider carrying more cash, and stop feeling broke when you pull your wallet from your pocket.

Make friends with people who make more money than you do — preferably much more money than you do. Take a millionaire to lunch and ask how he or she thinks about his or her business. Travel to places where wealth is abundant. Instead of taking the dirt-cheap trip to an out-of-the-way place in Mexico surrounded by the natives where you feel like a rich American, go where wealth accumulates. Pop down to the dealership and take a Porsche 911 for a test drive or the new Mercedes AMG SL. I could continue but I won't. I want to share a short conversation I had with Mark Victor Hansen, author of *Chicken Soup for the Soul* book dynasty. He told me during lunch he asked Tony Robbins one time why he was making hundreds of millions of dollars and Mark (at that time) was only making one to two-million dollars a year.

Tony responded with these questions: What's your mastermind group? Who are your professional and personal acquaintances?

When Mark said he spent time with others making approximately what he was currently earning, Tony replied, "That's why!" Because, as simple as that, Tony spends time with billionaires. That should cause you to think more!

Don't Be a Loser. Rise to the Occasion.

I'm sick and tired of seeing good business owners struggle financially, on a day to day basis. It's been frustrating in the past year to watch so many otherwise great people, accomplished businesspeople, and sincere entrepreneurs struggle financially. At least 25% of the industry went out of business during this prolonged recession. Others just struggle along making ends meet by working a day job while running their business at night or just sacrificing along the way and not running their business as much as they should (and often they could be doing something else altogether).

Don't get me wrong. The conversation among the consultants is "you can't fix losers" — that some people just won't rise to the occasion. It's also that the population skews 5%, 15%, 80% with 5% big winners, 15% winners, and 80% who'll just do little or nothing. Frankly, nothing I've seen contradicts these bleak assessments of human nature. However, I've also got to assume you are a 5% type or at least a top 20% in reality or potential, or you wouldn't be reading this, as 80% wouldn't bother.

Now to point out what may already be obvious to you. The transition to a winner as a business owner requires you move from being an employee or freelancer to actively taking charge and being an excellent leader who can lead by example, be an amazing salesperson to keep clients buying their services and products, educate their members of staff and market their own business effectively. By the way, you also must master at some level keeping track of your results (accounting and keeping stats), hiring and managing employees, and other administrative and management functions of your business along the way. This will make it easier in the long run if you get these admin and finance tasks out of the way. Keeping them near can help when you need information in the future.

The vast majority of the 80% types will never get to the successful business owner stage, nor master any of the other skills. Frankly, many never move beyond their development as an employee and end up failing as an owner of a business. Those types rebel against learning to be a salesperson (a big red flag as it is) and believe if you are a good enough as a business owner, then you don't need to "sell" your products or services as you will get enough revenue from clients by "word of mouth". Both are failure mentalities you must avoid at all costs. It's when you get trapped into these mindsets is when you can't see the forest for the trees, and you won't become the successful business owner you envision yourself to be.

The next pieces of advice I give you are some things you may already know, but they are very important to remember as you continue your pathway in business. The majority of your time and focus as a successful business operator must be on two things:

First, have *"raving fans"* among your client base. So, these aren't just any clients, they're not even just returning clients or ones you've retained throughout the years. These are the diamonds among the pebbles; they champion you and your business no matter what. They get involved with any fundraising you do, always comment and like on your social media platforms, always writing positive reviews and feedback for you to showcase and you can almost see them be part of the wider family of your business. This is the same for your employees; they are like a big extended family, led by you and your management team who truly is a 'product of the product', who show them and teach them leadership skills, life skills, and success skills. As an aside, it's difficult to teach people success skills if you don't have them yourself. It's why I've always focused more on teaching my staff life skills than on having specific scripts for them to parrot in different situations when they are representing the brand of my company.

Second, most of your time and effort, if (and only if) you are developing *"raving fans"*, must be spent on marketing. You must be constantly thinking about and working on how you get more new clients buying products and investing in your business. If you are developing "raving fans" and sharing life-changing skills with your customers, then you must be a "raging thunder lizard evangelist" for your program and insist your staff and clients are as well.

On this point, there are a couple of issues. What marketing effort will you master? And, how many ways can you implement to get new clients? It's important to have a few things you truly master to generate new clients and it's important to always have a "Parthenon" of marketing activities. In other words, 10 or more different ways you are attracting new clients each month. Never rely on just one mechanism.

The broad categories for attracting new clients might include:

1. Internal Promotional Activities.

This is anything (depending on your industry, that is) from fundraising activities, birthday parties, cake sales, etc. There are many reasons behind this and can be created to bring in more family members who will then purchase add-ons (i.e. mom, dad, sister, brother, wife, husband) or referrals. I've seen businesses master one or several mechanisms for referrals who can fill their business with only referral activities.

One friend has been fabulous at VIP offers for VIP clients, mostly generated by a membership or loyalty scheme for our customers. Making a big deal out of their loyalty will make them feel appreciated, so they are more likely to recommend their friends and family. Also, it makes for a fantastic layer to add to your social media marketing plan.

Another friend (Steve Doyon) has done a fabulous job hosting a huge number of fundraising events at his business and using that as a mechanism to convert attendees to immediate introductory clients and to add the rest to a fabulous follow-up sequence (mail, calls, email). This converts a huge number anywhere from week one to month 24 or beyond.

2. Community Outreach Activities.

This can range from business advice talks (or my original version, *"Gym Teacher for the Day"*) to programs with other businesses, the local community, etc. The marketing crowd calls this "host-parasite" relationships.

However, for our purposes, it's all about finding a crowd of *your* prospective clients and finding the best way(s) to introduce your business to that group.

3. Advertising.

This is anywhere you pay for media. It ranges from direct mail to targeted lists to newspaper advertising. I've set out to master every facet of this and have driven huge volumes to my business through newspaper advertising, newspaper inserts, direct mail, marriage mail (Val-Pak, Money Mailer, etc.), television — short form (30-second spots and long-form (infomercials) — and internet marketing (search engine optimization, site development, and pay-per-click).

4. Publicity.

This is finding ways to attract television stations, radio stations, and your local newspapers to feature your business or your customers in stories. At different times and in different markets each advertising mechanism can be effective. Over the years I've had from moderate to huge success with all of these. The trick with it is to look into every method, understand what it's used for and who it reaches (you wouldn't post on social media if your target demographic is elderly).

Many business owners during the past 10 years became convinced advertising doesn't work or isn't effective, so they cut it out of the budget. In that they are wrong. However, it is my opinion you should develop your marketing efforts by mastering community outreach and mastering internal promotional efforts (which become useful only at 100 to 150 active clients anyway).

To conclude on this subject, let me add a brief note about the internet. Keep in mind you've got to think of the internet by its sub-components.

First, your website for your customers. It's a resource that's different than your 'B2B' or 'Business to Business' content. This website shows the customer who you are, the events you have on, what you sell, why it's beneficial to them, where you can buy what you're selling and the next steps to purchase said items. That section of your website is designed to help with the "Raving Fans" component.

Second, is the website for prospects. I've rarely seen this done well. The site for prospects has a very limited purpose: to take a high percentage of visitors and convince them to share contact information with you (name, email, phone, mailing address), then to take a high percentage of those visitors and convince them to schedule a free or paid introductory taster or trial for a service, or a discount on a product your business provides. Your purpose is the same as an info call. They need to know little or nothing about you, your business, your style, your services, your products or your visions and values unless it facilitates them giving you contact information and scheduling a taster or trial.

Finally, the internet is media: it has several components designed to drive clicks — that is, prospects clicking a link to arrive at your prospect website. You can drive clicks through search engine optimization and pay-per-click advertising — in other words coming up on the first few pages of the search results when someone searches the proper keywords.

These two options are the modern equivalent of the Yellow Pages, being found quickly when someone is looking for the services your business provides. You can buy banners, articles, videos and other more traditional advertising methods to be in front of people who may be good prospects but are not looking for you. Many traditional media outlets are trying (and mostly failing) to get this to work.

The search engine and pay-per-click marketing approaches are well proven on the internet if there are adequate numbers of people looking for what you offer. The other more traditional advertising forms are yet to be proven on the internet but soon may work well, either normally online or through smart-phones or other mechanisms.

Recommendations to My Coaching Clients You Can Use

I want to share with you a few of the recommendations I have made to my coaching clients. They likely apply equally well to your situation.

First: Use a 3rd Party Companies When You Can

Many of you use too many methods to chase pennies and ignore dollars. For example in the martial arts industry monthly payments are common from clients so it's imperative to use a 3rd party company to collect these payments) A) It saves you effort, B) It separates you from the "money" in your clients' perspective and C) you'll make more money because that's their job.

This kind of company is available for medical professionals (or anyone who deals with insurance), in the legal field and in many other businesses.

This is just one example - find 3rd parties who can do tasks cheaper, better and improve your margins!

Second: Pricing, Programs, and Value

Rule of Thumb: You should targeting a specific income per client in your business. It's probably too low right now. Some key points to think about...

Can you build in recurring billing? Is there opportunity for your client to pay for a regular update or for consistent service? Recurring billing is a way you can sell "one time" and have it continue forever.

Pricing: Your price point in almost any business can be increased. Price, absent other criteria, determines perception of value. This means that higher prices (except in commodities like oil, gold, etc.) will be perceived as higher status in clients mind. Which is more valuable – a Porsche or a Subaru? There are models of each with the same performance yet the Porsche commands a higher price.

Levels of Service: You should look to offer more levels of service in your business. In the martial arts industry, an advanced program may be 50% to 100% more than a beginner program. In your business where are these opportunities to increase service levels / status / value and charge more to increase income per client?

Third: Expectations

Many of my coaching clients aspired to make $25,000 to $40,000 a month. The current standard is $80,000-or more per month in revenue. If you are struggling for small increases — or fighting the basic system — then it's time to adapt my strategy.

Fourth: The Mythology of business

Forget about how great you think your style is and how awesome your name is, your business won't pay your bills if you think:

- The market cares about your previous jobs or professional résumé.
- Your 10 or 20 years as a failing business has positioned you well for the future.
- Going it alone or doing things your way is a great idea.

During the last couple of months, there's been a lot of time wasted on one-on-one calls with business owners with $7,000 to $15,000 businesses who brag about how long they've been in business, their ads, their knowledge or their great curricula. Several of them, who haven't done much two or three months later, complain they need more of my time one-on-one.

Here are some of my favorite quotes for you to write down and remember:

"Winners remember results—losers remember reasons." (Source unknown)

"Most people would rather have a good excuse than good results." (I heard this one from Dan Kennedy, quoting someone else.)

"But when I said that nothing had been done, I erred in one important matter. We had committed ourselves and were halfway

out of our ruts. We had put down our passage money — booked a sailing to Bombay. This may sound too simple but is great in consequence. Until one is committed, there is hesitancy, the chance to draw back, always ineffectiveness. Concerning all acts of initiative (and creation), there is one elementary truth, the ignorance of which kills countless ideas and splendid plans: that the moment one commits oneself, their providence moves too. A whole stream of events issues from the decision, raising in one's favor all manner of unforeseen incidents, meetings, and material assistance, which no man could have dreamt would have come his way. I learned a deep respect for one of Goethe's couplets:

'Whatever you can do or dream you can begin it.

Boldness has genius, power, and magic in it.'"

W. H. MURRAY IN THE SCOTTISH HIMALAYA EXPEDITION, 1951.

The accurate Goethe quote is:

> *Then indecision brings its delays,*
> *And days are lost lamenting over lost days.*
> *Are you in earnest? Seize this very minute.*
> *What you can do, or dream you can do,*
> *begin it.*
> *Boldness has genius, power and, magic in it.*

Fifth: Know Your Business Statistics!

You must gather and maintain your operational and business statistics and know your current situation every week. Are you on target to achieve your daily, weekly, monthly, quarterly and yearly goals? How many clients do you need per day, week and month to match your projections? How many renewals/upgrades do you need? What is your target client retention rate? What are your daily break-even costs and daily profit goal?

Many business owners don't know their basic statistics, such as intros or first meetings, conversion rates, upgrades, new monthly payments or contract amounts — and they should.

If I asked you: "What are your totals for the month to date?" Would you have to refer to a ledger or computer, or ask someone? If you do then you have a problem.

Sixth: You Can't Do Anything Without New Clients.

Your target must always be 20 or more new clients per month — every month — or 240 new clients as a minimum every year, forever. If you have plenty of cash flow, then educate yourself about copywriting, TV, radio and direct mail. Improve your marketing skills and spend more time on grassroots promotional efforts and internal marketing. My record is 35 new clients (12-month contracts, signed and down payments, collected by EFT) in one day, back-to-back. It was an amazing feeling.

I remember an otherwise intelligent business owner who joined my coaching program — with the intent of earning $60,000 to $90,000 a year in income, which is a reasonable goal, considering many business owners in my coaching program can earn similar amounts. During the first month in my coaching program, the new member sent me a barrage of emails, stating among other things:

"I'm not willing to do contracts" and "I don't believe in 'upgrade or renewal' systems."

Geez. Why not just email me the following message?

"I have decided to take a permanent 'vow of poverty'. I will only be in this position of my business for the fun and fulfillment of working with my clients. I have absolutely no expectation of making more than a meager income, even though I've devoted much of my life to learn and master the skill set I have."

It amazes me otherwise intelligent human beings will decide to ignore intelligent business practices due to ignorance or the "unscrupulous" application of otherwise valid business systems by some operators.

If you remember nothing else, then please remember the four things every intelligent and rich business owner knows:

- Excellent customer service and retention are essential for long-term success.

- Aggressive renewal and upgrade systems account for 60-75% of all revenue of a successful business.
- You will greatly improve your understanding of some of the fundamentals of "how millionaires create 75% of their incomes", but I encourage you to keep an open mind and approach your business practices with both enlightened self-interest and the highest levels of integrity.
- Most business owners who join my coaching program generated an average of $15,000 to $17,000 in gross income per month; however, after eight to 12 months of working together, that average dramatically increased to $45,000 to $50,000 per month. Be aware this three-fold increase is not magical; it requires your willingness to 'empty the cup' and immediately apply intelligent, proven business systems to an otherwise quality program.

Wow, Extreme Success Academy!

I just got back from San Diego. Wow, what a great event. Our surprise guest was a blast from the past Andrew Wood. He was, as usual, fabulous on Saturday night. The obvious difference between the 'winners' and 'losers' starts with showing up. Everyone at the event learned enough to add $10,000.00 or more to their monthly revenue (in some cases much, much more) in the next 90 days if they implement what they learn. Several members I talked with have doubled their revenue using what they learned at Extreme Success Academy last year in San Antonio! That is a serious recession — imagine what would have happened in 'boom times'.

As you would have expected, Brian Tracy was fabulous as always and shared some great insights both into his background and experiences, as well as into what you must do to maximize your results and grow your business. Frankly, the entire roster was brimming with such fabulous information it's hard to know where to start. I'm told I changed many people's thinking on Friday and Sunday about how an operator should think and about what it takes to move to the highest levels of our profession. Toby Milroy gave a ton of "meat and potatoes" information all day Friday to start everyone off strong. Many folks commented on the huge value they received (as always) on the nuts and bolts of effective grass-roots marketing efforts.

Please, Please, Permit Me to FAIL!

I t's just amazing to me how aggressively some people will argue with you when you are trying to help them be successful — they are arguing for failure. If you've studied much of Tony Robbins' materials, he talks about "my delusion" — meaning he believes his goals are achievable and external events will help not hurt his progress. You can have the opposite delusion —everything external is conspiring against you. Your belief system, either way, will conspire to make sure you get what you expect.

It goes back to the great quote:

"Most people would rather have a good excuse than good results."

Here's a recent e-mail I received (I won't share with you the name, for obvious reason).

"... your numbers have a snowball's chance in hell down here. In case you haven't heard, Arizona has not only the second-worst foreclosure rate in the country but is now the second poorest state in the union! Only Louisiana beat us for the top spot! Sometimes you remind me of Nero watching Rome burn. I know you are trying to help but castigating me for not showing "your" numbers are not only frustrating but counterproductive.

"There are no down payments because people can't/won't pay them.

"Zero PIFs because nobody has that kind of money. Despite what we show them we have and can do, most simply walk down the street to the next little TKD hole-in-the-wall and sign up for $50/month.

"$99/month is considered "expensive" here in Tucson...especially with a contract which scares the crap out of people."

Anytime you say or believe that nobody can do something, you're wrong. Someone can and someone will. If you say people won't pay something, you are probably just reviewing your belief system not the reality of the market. It's easy to conclude the economy sucks, and frankly, if you watch the news or listen to popular opinion, it's a reasonable conclusion. However, such externalization of the blame for results does nothing to improve your income or your overall results.

A consideration is the demographics of income issues. Approximately nationally, a person who is 30-plus years of age, with an education level of college or better, has an unemployment rate of less than 4.5%. That same person with not a lot of education, less than 30 years old, is close to 20%.

Therefore, targeting white-collar, educated parents is vital for marketing success, both for income and employment purposes. Single, young adult males are the absolute worst in the current environment as a market target, but again this depends on who your demographic is in the first place.

As an economist by educational background (BA Economics, MBA) I always feel compelled to investigate and evaluate comments such as this to see if there is, in fact, a kernel of truth buried in it.

It's easy to look externally for an excuse, but I'd suggest we fix your systems and processes from the inside out. What must you do? Target the right audience, those who are likely to both values your program and be willing and able to pay for it.

Market extensively throughout targeted areas in your community and draw from communities with the income and stability you need for your business. Then, continually upgrade the quality of your program to increase its value to your clients and prospective clients.

The Quickest Way to Kill a Business

I t's rather simple: The quickest way to kill a business is to become good at sales and marketing without mastering the service and education aspects.

Let me say that again, differently. If you are not an excellent employer, salesperson, leader, and motivator, then the absolute worst thing you can do is expose your business to a huge number of prospective clients, so your community learns about how poor your business delivers this critical service.

Let me give you this example from a couple of other industry perspectives. Dan Kennedy is one of the many "marketing gurus" I've studied. He shares a story about opening a new restaurant. After exploring all of the many advertising options — Val-Pak, money mailer, flyer, direct mail, etc. — the restaurant owners decided to print certificates, instead, good for a free meal (absolutely free — not two for one, no cost for drinks, etc.). These certificates were delivered to every home and office in the restaurant's immediate vicinity by hand, with a personal invitation to try the restaurant.

The restaurant was swamped with traffic during its first month, with very little revenue, because it gave away the lion's share of the meals. What do you think happened next? If this were as much of the story I knew, my first answer would probably be there is no business the second month, or thereafter, and the restaurant quickly closes. My second answer is that during the second month, it would be just as busy, with happily paying customers; and the restaurant's business quickly grows from there. What's the difference? By now it should be obvious: good food and fast, friendly service.

If the restaurant had good food and fast-friendly service, then its expensive marketing effort was well worth it. If not, then the management just proved to everyone in its neighborhood the restaurant was not worth revisiting for a free meal or any other reasons.

How about another example? One of my executive staff members worked for a branded oil-change business for many years. It's the best strategy to grow a new location was the same as explained above. The company would distribute certificates widely that were good for a free oil change, with no strings attached.

Once many of its neighbors visited the location and were treated professionally and courteously with quality service, they were very likely to return again and again for service but paying the standard rate. Again, this strategy would backfire quickly for a poorly run location.

What if the location was poorly maintained, with a grumpy member of staff who performed the service poorly and looked up a female customer's skirt while changing the oil? The word would spread quickly, but not positively. The company would be ensured a tough launch, and have difficulty overcoming its bad reputation.

The business industry has experienced this situation often enough that many excellent entrepreneurs, who are also excellent teachers and mentors to their employees are afraid of developing their marketing talent or sales skills for fear of becoming like those other 'shady operators'.

In contrast, I would say the two biggest sins are first, quality business people who are afraid of or unwilling to learn to promote their business and grow their client base; and second, lousy business people who master the art of marketing and sales and, therefore, poison the customer experience for their clients. No business ever thrived without mastering three key functions: marketing, sales and service delivery. Miss any one of these key areas and you are doomed to financial failure.

I highly recommend you start with a top-to-bottom overview of your business. Forget, for the moment, the mastery of your chosen art. It's not very relevant to your client's experience. Instead, you should focus on every aspect of your service delivery, starting with the most important, and then reviewing all the supporting areas. Start with your rapport with your customers and then look at your communications skills. Next, how are your business structures, your facilities, staff training, and customer support? How's the appearance of your key staff members and yourself? First impressions do count. After you've reviewed these areas, it's time to master the marketing and sales functions, and then grow your client base dramatically.

Important Issues for Large Operators

As your business expands, and you can no longer personally control every aspect of your operation, several important issues begin to arise you may never have previously considered.

The first of these I'd like to address is how to ensure control, as you develop a loyal client base and strong, skilled staff members. Once you expand to multiple locations or your single business increases to a large client base of 300 or 3000 or more depending on the type of business, you will find it necessary to delegate much, or perhaps all, of the managerial duties to an employee. In business, personal loyalty and respect for the owner and management team is an important component of your developmental process. Many businesses depend on a strong hierarchy and obedience to the management team and owner.

The same structure that helped you maintain order in the early stages of your growth can become a problem as you grow if not managed properly. Horror stories abound, so be warned!

A common story is the development of a member of staff, they begin to show initiative and some real talent and enthusiasm, so you begin to train them up further. Once you feel they're competent enough, you may allow them to begin training up other members of staff who have shown potential as well. If they teach and inspire for long enough, he becomes a cornerstone if your business; they're highly respected, so you offer them a career with you. He's doing most of the training and eventually, he gains a management position. This enables you to focus more on the sales, marketing and administrative aspects of your business.

Gradually, your employees begin recognizing your star employee as their primary mentor, and the mentor starts to take great pride in "his" employees' achievement.

What comes next is this employee often begins to hear from clients he should have his own business. Perhaps he marries and his wife continually complains he should have his own business and he's not being paid enough; and, of course, he is responsible for the success of the business since all the owner does is sit in the office and talk to people all day.

Then one day, like a lightning bolt from the blue...

You can probably finish the story. I've seen cases where your previously loyal employee has moved across the street, followed by letters and phone calls to solidify the solicitation of your clientele.

The question becomes, how do you protect yourself from such a disaster? There are many ways business owners attempt to protect themselves — and this can be applied in any area of business. What doesn't work is always to be your staff member's primary contact and work aggressively to make sure you are always seen as the top leader, teacher and main contact. That approach is fine when you have a relatively small team but then you must delegate authority and let others take some responsibility. What must happen then, are several things. First, your business must be built on a formal hierarchy, with you visible at the top. It must always be clear you are the senior person in your business and all others report to you. This is where larger organizations and affiliations often help to solidify everyone's relative position.

Second, before hiring anyone, it is important to have a clear understanding. The written understanding must include several points:

- Your enthusiasm about helping your employees develop a substantial career.
- Your willingness to help them grow in any way possible.
- Your willingness to compensate continually their relative contribution to the financial outcome of your business.
- Their commitment to supporting now and always you and your business.
- Their understanding it is unacceptable to ever teach any of your staff members outside of the business environment. Regardless of how the future unfolds, they will never solicit any of your members of staff or your clients for that matter for a service similar to your current one.
- Their understanding that it is acceptable for them to open a business in the future under your banner or independently, but

they will not open it within a reasonable distance, so as not to compete with you, or you to compete with them.

In conclusion, there are many landmines to avoid as your business grows. Developing your competition is certainly one it is important to control and monitor.

We're in a Simple Business.

I remember while working on the MBA (Master's in Business Administration) thinking about what a simple business is, and what it would look like in reality. During one of the classes within the program, we were working on multivariate scheduling programs (how to program traffic lights in London or schedule flights for United Airlines) and then Pert Charts, Gantt Charts and things like that. The next class was all about managerial accounting — determining the costs of a product by allocating overhead by machine hours and the like.

A couple of things dawned on me then. First, a business can be simple, no matter what any of those 'business gurus' have stated. Second, many business owners who struggle, do so by over-complicating their business and confusing simplicity with a lack of sophistication — or, confusing complexity with substance.

It's important to keep in mind there are three vital primary drivers of your business: getting clients, client renewal and client retention. If what you are working on during any given moment does not directly impact attracting new clients, renewing existing clients or keeping existing clients for a longer period, then you are wasting your time.

Take those three "drivers" and overlay your pricing and structure, and you have all the key elements to increase (or decrease) your gross revenue. In my efforts with consulting, I'm often confronted with business owners who are busy confusing activity with accomplishment, or who have over-complicated their life and their business by ignoring the basic premise above.

In practice, how does this work? One way is to determine what products and services you are going to offer as part of your business. The first question is always: "Will these products encourage customers to stay longer with our program or will it accelerate attrition?" If you reasonably expect any piece of your service to improve your overall client retention, then consider it. Next, ask yourself if it can be used to enhance renewals. This is often something new or different is a marvelous hook for the renewal.

I've made this mistake occasionally. The most important to remember is you are not your market. What you are excited to learn has little or nothing to do with what will be a nice addition to improve retention or to be an attractive addition to enhance renewals. Throughout the last 30 years, I've seen many, many cycles of adding new, exciting products or services (or pretending to do so) hoping to attract more clients.

There are times when media trends lead to a big upsurge in different products and services. One point is you should first pick a target market and then decide what to offer that target market so it will be receptive to want to purchase from you and paying a reasonable price for your products or services.

The next point is that in most cases, there will be a lot of instances where clients approach you and do so from a point of near or total ignorance about your business and the industry it's in. Never assume your level of knowledge about your areas of expertise when approaching a market. They may use a current buzz word but frankly, they seldom know really what they want. It's up to you to help them home in on what they want and why.

Third, evaluate each media trend and ask: "Is this driving a surge of people looking to pay for the service or product I offer?"

You will make huge headway in your business by focusing on the three drivers and avoiding anything that distracts. The most successful businesses I see (at the "bottom line") focus on one type of service or type of product. They add to or enhance what they offer based upon having more resources, more training so they can entice client renewals and keep their services interesting and relevant to their target demographic. They focus on their "bread and butter", their target, creating $30,000, $50,000, $80,000 or more monthly revenue from one type of service or product. They constantly work on improving their customer experience while expanding their reach into their immediate community.

If the focus is on the adult audience, they get better and better at attracting that target audience. If their focus is on the kids' market, then they get better and better at retaining kid customers. Most successful businesses do not try to attract all markets; one offsets the other. It would be like seeing a combination of McDonald's, Morton's and Chilies. They're all different target audiences, different branding, different facilities, and different approaches.

Critical Success Skill: Build Immunity to Criticism

Here's a business tip you must learn — and learn well.

Recently, I "googled" the name of my business on the Internet, just to learn if anyone was misusing the name or stealing my content, which is considered "intellectual property" nowadays. Can you believe this happens? It sure does. Here's what I found.

Some businesses have copied the contents directly from my websites — word for word. Often, the perpetrators are so blatant they even use my name and our testimonials. This is a very clear case of plagiarism. Keep in mind you're allowed to copy concepts, but you are not allowed to duplicate/steal the text or the pictures/images from anyone or any business.

The important point is to build your business to a professional level requires you do two things:

- Systematize and professionalize, which will create a more consistent customer experience and a higher quality operation.
- Ignore the idiots who don't understand why you are successful. Learn to build immunity to criticism. It's a critical skill to be successful.

Marketing your Business: The Key Is Repetition

Keep in mind an advertising rule of thumb: until you have exposed a prospective client to your message at least seven times, he or she doesn't understand what you are trying to communicate.

It often works in this manner: a mother in your target audience glances at your ad in a local newspaper. The headline is somewhat interesting, however, the phone rings, her kid spills his milk or one of the thousands of other potential distractions catch the mom's attention and she forgets your ad.

A postcard from your business is delivered to her family's mailbox. She glances at your postcard while she sorts the mail into two stacks. Pile A is personal correspondence, bills, etc., which she must keep. Pile B is junk mail and other non-requested materials she typically throws in the trash. Your postcard is discarded too, but it has had a minor impact on her mind and some vague familiarity of having seen your ad before.

The neighbor pulls into the driveway and her five-year-old hops from the car, which sparks a vague memory about a conversation with the child's mother about a business they've bought from recently and have had a good experience with. She still can't remember the conversation or the name of the business.

Glancing through the local paper, she sees your ad again. This time it looks a little familiar. The headline seems targeted at her. She reads most of the body copy and decides to discuss it with her partner. This is quickly forgotten when she needs to manage 10 other daily crises before her spouse arrives home after work.

A friend at the gym mentions she had fantastic service from your business; she loves the brand. It's now a familiar name to her.

Another flyer or postcard from your business appears in her mailbox. This time, during her mail sorting, she saves your letter in the "A" pile. She glances at the contents and thinks it looks interesting. She decides to investigate this idea and the letter is attached to the refrigerator to be discussed later. Nothing happens yet, though.

The next-door neighbor's kid comes home again the following day. Remembering the name of your business from the conversation with the child's mother, she expresses interest in knowing more about her experience. The child of the first mother now knows the firsthand account of one of your customer's experience.

The mother then finds your third promo letter in her mailbox. This time, the letter is placed by phone. She calls your business that same day. If you've trained a staff member to answer the phone professionally, then he or she schedules an appointment for the mother to come into your store to find out more about what you can offer them. When they do come into the store and your charismatic members of staff help them with their questions, build rapport with the wife and her spouse, present your services effectively and keep their attention, then they will become a customer.

Remember, when tracking your results try to determine not only why the prospect called today, but also how they learned about your business originally — and all of the materials they've seen. It helps you to determine what type of advertising is best for your business. Whatever advertising or promotional medium you choose to use determines how to expose prospects to your message a minimum of three times and, preferably, seven to 10 times.

A Dumb Statement!

A coaching client of mine had resulted in an increase in his revenues from $17,000 to more than $30,000 a month. The methods he used to grow his business are those he learned from a one-on-one consultation and attending a Boot Camp. He never attended any of our other mastermind sessions or took advantage of many other opportunities I provided. He then decided once his gross doubled there was nothing more to learn. He had learned one or two secrets and was done.

Dumb, that was a dumb move. What could he have accomplished? For starters, he could have increased his revenues from $50,000 to $75,000 to $100,000 a month. Maybe he thought he knew everything I knew — frankly, he hadn't even scratched the surface. Maybe he thought he knew enough. It seems stupid to me to "leave money on the table".

Unfortunately, there are many business owners who, once they hit revenue numbers, they thought were impossible, and then lose perspective. They suffer from one of two syndromes:

The legend-in-their-own-mind syndrome: Suddenly, they've decided that they know so much that they should be the "guru" and learn no more. That's a dangerous egotism that must be avoided at all costs.

The second syndrome is just as dangerous: They decide they've "arrived" at the "top" and know everything they need to run and maintain their businesses. A successful business can never be static, and a successful business owner can never be satisfied with the status quo. I've completely reinvented my business at least every seven years, and I did so once again this spring. Once you stop evolving, you die. Our industry is constantly changing—and so should your preparations and expectations. My expectations have changed dramatically over the past 25 years. What would have seemed an unbelievable gross revenue 13 years ago now seems a rather mundane net profit this year and the pace is accelerating. Don't become comfortable or think you have nothing more to learn.

"Entrepreneurial Seizures" and Other E-Myths

Gerber in *The E-Myth* described all businesses are started by a technician who one day had an "entrepreneurial seizure" and went from being a technician to a business owner. He describes the phenomenon of new business owners who think the technical aspect of their business is going to encompass the majority of their business who are discouraged and dismayed to discover they have to wear multiple 'hats'. They suddenly discover that they must be the head of HR (Human Resources,) Marketing Director, Sales Manager, CFO (Chief Financial Officer,) and on and on — all of which have little or nothing to do with baking cakes or repairing cars.

In our case I like to make it a little simpler; 90-95% of our time as a business owner is focused on three outcomes:

1.) New Client acquisition

2.) Client Retention

3.) Renewals or Upgrades.

If you are considering doing something new to help or develop your business, ask yourself first if it will help you get more clients, keep them longer, or move them into more expensive subscriptions or services.

That having been said, it's important to recognize you as the owner (and any full-time staff you have) will likely spend as much time focused on marketing efforts as on teaching. I always teach my staff to build a rapport with the clients who pass through the door. It's all about what we can offer them, as opposed to who we are and what we do, so it's best to have the customer's best interests at heart. You, as a business owner, should focus on personal rapport with clients, looking for opportunities to retain them; concentrate on goals and client interaction for long-term achievement (renewals), and focus on an introductory taster to your services, conferences, add-ons and generating referrals. So, to summarize a couple of things before moving on:

Mistakes broke business owners make:

- Spending more time on personal training within your field, such as writing or fixing cars (which is good to a certain extent) rather than learning and training in sales, marketing, and advertising.
- Delegating sales and marketing (hiring a Program Director).
- Deciding they are "not a salesperson" and therefore they won't learn more communication and sales skills.
- Showing up at the office later than your employees say 10 a.m. or 11 a.m., and staying until around 4 p.m. This works out to only be around 16-20 hours a week, which your employees will notice as you're not putting in the time and effort they do.
- Implementing only one or two things a month to attract new clients.

Ironically, it's true most business owners would rather sit in their business broke and slowly (or, quickly) going out of business rather than leave the office and go find new clients. You've got to be willing to get out into your community and connect with people and organizations who can help you fill your business.

The traits of a successful business owner are:

- They treat their business as a full-time, lucrative career. They set their alarm, get out of bed and go to work promoting their business.
- They understand a business is as much about marketing, sales, and customer service as it is about proficiency in the specialist field.
- They extensively invest in their education in each of the key areas of their business including sales, marketing, teaching methodology, hiring/training/supervising employees, personal goal setting and motivation among others.
- They network with other successful business owners and avoid hanging out with unsuccessful owners. This is so they can get some good tips from someone who has that experience.

- They keep track of all the key statistics to monitor their business.

Admittedly, neither list is extremely comprehensive, but you get the basic idea.

Back to the Program Director comment. I've seen very few single or multi-branch business owners who are the full-time head of staff who work ridiculous hours to ensure their business is running smoothly. One of the first staff positions they tend to fill is first a part-time, then a full-time head employee. It's a bad idea in most cases to first hire someone to "take care of sales". First, you should master every function of your business before hiring someone else to do it for you. You must be on top of the key skills to teach them or to delegate them.

With business owners I work with, most who are grossing $10,000 or under are teaching, working those long hours for most of the time. The owners who are grossing $20,000 to $50,000 a month are focusing on marketing, selling and customer service primarily. Most over $50,000 a month or with multiple locations spend their time training and supervising staff rather than doing the selling themselves. That having been said, I've seen businesses up to $100,000 a month where the owner handles most of, or even all the sales processes.

Anyway, to conclude it's vital you are constantly investing in your training and development in all aspects of your business operation. You likely need to focus first on marketing and sales as a primary study.

Next, you need to realize you are ultimately in a selling and marketing business. You'll need to invest more training and time in implementation on those functions than you've invested already in your training for development. Most business owners think nothing of training seven to 10 hours a week on their physical skills but, fail to invest an equal amount of time on improving their career and income.

Move into the top 20%, then the top 5%, and ultimately into the top 1% by developing your business, teaching, sales and marketing skills every day.

Focus Your Marketing Dollars on a Specific Target Audience

I remember a long talk I had with Bill Clark, followed by similar conversations with Lloyd Irvin and Jeff Smith. We all agreed on the following.

My conversation with Bill Clark was focused on the misadventures of many businesses that should be marketing the benefits they offer to specific markets. Your business must be clearly in a category and your marketing dollars focused on a specific target market.

So, there's a business nearby that sells similar services to mine, but he's incorporated a kids' development program and I've created our "building successful kids" program and extensive character development and leadership program for kids and families.

Both of us have claimed territory and developed a clear image of what we do. Our focus is on kids, families and character development. At the other end of the spectrum are other types of businesses that are clearly and unabashedly targeting the young adult male market.

The commonality of these businesses doing very well is based on several factors. One of those factors is deciding whom you are targeting and, in essence, "the side of the industry you've chosen" and then being very clear about your position and very focused on your market.

Many other business owners should think about one of my favorite lines from an otherwise forgettable movie (The Stepfather): "Wait a minute, who am I here?" Those who fail, try to be all things to all people. Those who succeed focus on being very good at what a segment of the market wants to learn.

Marketing Your Business: Media and Promotional Activities

Here are a few questions which will help you decide where to spend your dollars, time and energy on marketing, advertising or promotional efforts.

Is the marketing campaign or promotion targeted specifically for your business? (This question addresses geography).

Does a demo or ad attract too many people who have not qualified prospects for my business or is it targeted directly to your neighborhood? (Addressing people.)

Are the people who will see the demo or read the ad your exact target prospects? (Addressing income.) You can spend your time doing demos at business events, but I'd rather present to specific target audiences instead. Make sure you aren't sending flyers to retirement homes and expecting clientele if they aren't your target demographic.

I've wasted plenty of time doing free sessions for those who can't currently afford my programs. I'm all for contributing to the community; however, a better alternative is to grow your business to 500 clients and gross $50,000-plus per month, and then donate 5% or 10% to charities instead.

Focus and Responsiveness

Will the audience pay attention to your ad? Is the publication where your ad runs a free newspaper that lands in mailboxes or driveways unsolicited and remains unread or a subscription periodical your audience is more likely to read and see your ad? Are you on the sidelines during a demo or promotional activity, hoping someone will talk with you or are you the main event?

Is your presentation "laser-focused?" Too many business owners think: "There will be people of all ages and types in the audience, so I will create a generic presentation [letter, ad, demo], so it applies to everyone." This is a big mistake! Trying to be everything to everyone is being nothing to no one.

It's much better to "rifle shot" your advertising that is very appealing to 5% or 15% of your general audience and ignore the majority. During your demo, highlight one aspect of your program targeted to the most likely prospects in the audience. Don't present so many points no one will remember any of them; instead, always focus on one target market at a time.

Entertainment, Education, and Persuasion

Trying to entertain your audience is a huge temptation in presentations and advertising. Entertainment is always interesting; however, it doesn't persuade the audience to participate.

For example, when I saw the acclaimed stage show Riverdance, I had great seats, enjoyed the show and was amazed at the choreography, lighting, and talent. It was a wonderful night of entertainment; however, personally, it did nothing to inspire me to learn Irish dancing. The theater was charging $35 to $75 per seat, and 2,500-plus seats (the theater's capacity) were sold — six times a week.

I know why they were doing the show and it had nothing to do with motivating audience members to become dancers. Don't imitate the theater and the show's methods unless you can do $125,000 at the gate per night.

It's great to educate your audience about the value of participating in your activity or service, why they should participate and what they will experience as clients. Again, think in terms of targeting your audience, and teaching them the benefits of participating in your program.

The education you provide must be about "what's in it for them" — and not about you, your style, its history, why it's better than other styles, etc. They just don't care about any of that stuff.

Customers generally don't take an interest in what your business provides because of a history lesson, your style or the prestige of your grandmaster. They purchase from you because they expect some benefit and believe you'll be concerned and capable enough to provide that benefit.

Capturing the "Slight Edge"

I'd like to share an important success secret understood by Bill Gates, Donald Trump and most all self-made millionaires and billionaires. First, though, a little personal background is necessary.

During recent months, I've been to four major marketing, management or Internet-marketing boot camps or multi-day seminars. The total cost was much more than $10,000, not including travel, hotels, meals and rental cars. Additionally, I just ordered approximately $1,100 in audio CD programs, books or reference materials related to my business and personal growth.

During the past 27 years, I've done plenty of reading and studying, and spent much time in formal and informal management, teaching, sales, marketing, and human relations education. In addition to my MBA degree, I've spent thousands of hours learning about how to run a business and teach people effectively.

The truth is I have so much information that I leave some of the seminars that I've attended empty-handed, because there was nothing left for me to buy. Like other multi-million-dollar entrepreneurs in the same situation, we already owned all the content, and want more.

Why, then, would I still invest in education and development at this elite level? That's the success secret. It's called the "Slight Edge".

Here's another example for you: Years ago, I remember sitting in rapt attention as Joe Lewis explained the minute details of his renowned sidekick. At that time, I had the best kicks of those with whom I trained and, frankly, I knew quite a bit about how to execute a sidekick. That wasn't just my opinion. Jeff Smith and John Chung and many others whose opinions I respected also shared that opinion.

Why did I pay such close attention to Joe Lewis? Because he had one of the most powerful sidekicks ever. He had developed subtle distinctions about his sidekick and how he executed it that was way beyond my understanding of that technique.

The other small business owners who fail or achieve just slightly beyond mediocrity will consider a book, CD, seminar or another learning opportunity as the content they've heard or read previously. Those who are very successful will look for the subtle distinctions in those materials or renew their commitment to gain new knowledge by studying the material.

Every month, I talk with business owners who gross $8,000 a month or less and business owners who gross $2 million or more a year. Frankly, it's not that the guys doing millions know 10 or 20 times more than the small business owners. It's that they've learned some subtle distinctions that helped them move to dramatically higher levels, and they've continued to remain open to and seek new material.

Learn new material every month; internalize content you've heard, but perhaps not mastered, and gain subtle distinctions to propel you to new heights and motivate you to even stronger implementation. You'll certainly benefit from the financial results!

Want Massive Profits? Implement a "Drip" System!

I was listening today to one of Tony Robbins' Power Talk CDs. Something he said struck a chord for me concerning what I see every day in our industry. To paraphrase, he said someone asked him what the difference was between when he was broke and now. He said the primary difference between when he was broke and now was a sense of urgency and positive expectations. What he was describing is a level of entrepreneurial urgency that's driven by a belief in the potential results. If you expect to fail, it's easy to adopt a "why bother" attitude.

Let's take just one example of this statement applied to businesses. An example I've repeated several times is the story of a chiropractor who added on average 35 new patients every month. When asked what to do to add 35 new patients per month he responded he didn't know anything to do to add 35 new patients, but he did know 35 things which would add one new patient or more.

I can't tell you how many business owners I've talked to who just don't do much to build their business. I'll ask them month after a month what they did in the past month to promote their business and they'll only name one or two things. I ask them for progress since the last month and they have a list of excuses for why they haven't started implementing the new marketing strategies they discussed the previous month. Months go by and they get little or nothing accomplished. Their online presence and marketing become stagnant and stale.

It's important to make sure you always have the entrepreneurial urgency that Robbins talks about. Always, always, always implement aggressively and immediately.

"A good plan violently executed now is better than a perfect plan executed next week."

George S. Patton

Frankly, most people are losers. They look for reasons to justify their failure rather than find the drive to succeed. All populations sort themselves into the top 5% (big winners), the top 20% (winners), and the bottom 80% (typically don't do much, look for excuses).

So, what's the biggest difference between the top 5% and the bottom 80%? Implementation with a sense of urgency. It's got to be done now, not next week, next month or next year.

To use Zig Ziglar's line — losers wait for all the lights to be green before heading across town. If you just set your alarm, got up, got out and talked to people one-to-one outside of your business every day for five hours, you'd practically be guaranteed to make $250,000 or more *net* in the coming year. Better still, would be a business with 500 customers or more.

Will you take action? I don't know. Frankly, it's up to you. We've given you every tool you need (and a bunch more than you need). However, if you think, ponder, worry, try to understand everything 100%, you'll get to next year at the same place — or worse.

Go implement; attract 100 more customers, renew customers with their subscriptions. It's good for $300,000 to $500,000 if nothing else. The bottom line? It's worth your time to set your alarm clock, get your staff out of bed and hit the ground running every day on marketing your business.

How do you get started? Frankly, every month we are giving you lots of tools. Each teleconference gives you a bunch of great ideas — you should never miss a call.

Internal Promotions to Create Add-ons and Referrals.

The best way to get add-ons is to be assumptive, especially with families and subscribing to your service. Is there something for everyone? Add family packages with discounts for the little ones, so the parents think nothing of it and realize it's a good deal for the kids.

The best way to consistently get referrals is from two main sources:

Hosting events at your office or store as it will be easy to invite friends to attend. These include (but are certainly not limited to):

- Birthday parties.
- Cake sales.
- Charity fundraising days.
- Host free workshops for people to learn about what

your business does.

The key in all of these is getting the RSVPs and/or name, address, phone, and email and following up 24 or more times in the coming 10 months. They may not become a customer this week but maybe in three, five or seven months.

Connecting with organizations who complement the services you offer, can provide a mutually beneficial partnership to both businesses and attract more customers for both companies. These include but certainly are not limited to:

- Finance companies
- Universities (for placements and internships)
- Local small businesses (support and referrals)

Remember, once you collect a lead, follow up — forever. Direct mail is a key. See below.

Suspects into Prospects ("Farming")

Find extremely targeted lists of "suspects", or "potential clients" and work that list consistently and repetitiously.

Examples:

Social media - posts that target your demographic and direct mail.

Step 1. Letter or Postcard #1, #2, #3, #4 (within six weeks)

Step 2. "Drip System"* Monthly Mailer — send forever.

Prospects into Intros

Example: Attended an event you hosted.

Step 1. Letter or postcard with telephone follow-up.

Step 2. Mailer #2, #3, #4 within six weeks.

Step 3. "Drip System" Monthly Mailer — Send forever.

Step 4. January, May, September: Mailer #1, #2, #3 weekly plus telephone follow-up.

Lost Intros into Customers

Example: Came to an event but never became a customer as you followed up but they canceled when called.

Step 1. A follow-up letter with lots of testimonials.

Step 2. "Price Drop Offer," i.e., one month free, three months for a bargain price, or 2-for-1 offer.

Step 3. Telephone call follow-up to "price drop offer."

Step 4. "Drip System" (Monthly Mailer) — send forever.

Step 5. (January, May, September) — Mailer #1, #2, #3 weekly plus telephone follow-up.

The Good Old Days That Never Were!

Maybe you, like me, remember the "good old days" when providing quality products for the customer and excellent customer service was the rule, not the exception, and you had to be dedicated and have incredible perseverance to build up a successful business with a loyal client base.

I remember my first few sales when my business was just starting up; it was a joyous occasion, I was anxious and hoped they liked what I was selling to them; it all went smoothly and from then, I haven't looked back. What's more important than reminiscing constantly is looking at the present and focusing on the following issues.

Focus Your Attention on These Issues

Sales
    Many business owners think 'sales' is a dirty word and openly rebel against learning effective sales or closing methods. Unfortunately, there's also been a group, during the last couple of years, which teaches only "high pressure" sales techniques and think they are the be-all and end-all of running a profitable business. The reality is a little different.

You cannot be a successful business owner without mastering marketing and selling methods appropriate to your business. You must also know "generic" or general, sales and marketing knowledge. You must be aware of how other businesses, especially businesses similar to yours, sell and market.

Dan Kennedy says you are committing "marketing incest" when you only learn sales and marketing from your industry. Just because a method is an industry norm doesn't mean it's the right or only way of doing business. At a minimum, you should watch how chiropractors, dentists, dance academies and many similar businesses market and sell themselves; I can almost guarantee you will learn something.

That having been said, long-term success in business is about customer service, long-term client retention, and quality referrals. You must be a well-respected and highly regarded by other businesses in your area, by educators, doctors, and other opinion leaders.

Mastering sales methodology without the focus on customer service and satisfaction will allow you to suck plenty of money from your community during the short run but ensure mediocrity or self-destruction in the long run.

Quality Customer Service
Many of the quality and service problems businesses experience are due to the industry being greatly personality-based. Many businesses I've

worked with don't have the best structures and content for the customers to understand and be completely happy with.

One of my top priorities in my learning during the 1980s was organizing the structure of processes. I hired a PhD educator, buried myself in the research and went to work.

While it's always important to have staff members who are personable and charismatic, much in the development of your client base can be addressed by saying the right thing at the right time and make sure you're providing the very best service and products you can.

The next area is creating systems which improve the client's perception of interest and concern.

Studies have been conducted on why people stop patronizing businesses. The leading factor, again and again, is not dissatisfaction with the quality of service received. The leading factor cited is "perceived apathy." What are you doing to make sure your client knows you believe they are valuable, and you are paying attention? Do you do that systematically or irregularly? Do clients "fall through the cracks"?

The tremendous improvement to the bottom line which can be achieved with only small improvements in long-term customer loyalty has also been scientifically studied and validated. Remember, you spend the most to acquire new clients. If it costs $500 or more to get a new client, then would it be worth similar investments in additional recognition to improve long-term retention?

I've seen a very small number of businesses do this very well. Most do not do it very well. The "sales-is-the-only-thing" trend in our industry leads business owners to believe that customer service doesn't matter. That is a tremendous disservice to everyone involved and a massive warning sign.

Back to Basics

Recently, I've seen much industry press coverage about "big businesses" that I would not consider successful. Keep in mind that there are always two factors that must be in place at any performance level to be considered successful.

First: Profit.

It doesn't matter what your gross revenues are unless you keep a reasonable percentage for the bottom line. Don't be seduced by a bigger-is-better mentality. Study the numbers below carefully. They are based on a 2,000 to 3,000-square-foot location with two full-time staff, one or both of which could be the business owner/operator.

Second: Sustainability.

One-month numbers may be impressive, but I'd rather see a big billing check that minimally covers 100% of your fixed monthly expenses and double that number regularly in total gross.

Definitions of Success:

Either in income or profit margins

Outstanding: $75,000 and more (50%+ Profit)

Successful: $50,000 to $74,000 (40%+ Profit)

Foundational: $30,000 to $49,000 (25%+ Profit)

Breakeven to Marginal: $18,000 to $29,000 (10% Profit)

Imperiled (on the brink of financial disaster): $17,900 or less. (Break even or negative cash flow)

In Marketing, What's Old is New Again

What's new? In the here and now, things are a lot different when it comes to marketing your business — but, no different than they ever were. OK, I know that's contradictory, but let me explain.

In marketing, social media is all the rage. Consultants and pundits are running around claiming the way the new world is to 'have a conversation' with your customers. The interesting thing about that is everything old is new again. In the 1960s, 1970s, and 1980s the important elements of running a business were to have a conversation with your customers. Honestly, for most service or retail businesses, no one had to create the internet or Facebook®, LinkedIn®, Ping® or whatever, to have a conversation with their customer.

Maybe if you are selling Doritos®, Pepsi®, Tide® or you're some other product company, creating a direct channel of communications with your customers without relying on the big retailers or whoever is selling your stuff is probably useful. However, in our case, you should be having a personal conversation with your customers quite often — probably a few times a week.

There is, after all, a lesson there. The product we have is more about the rapport you create with your customers. It's about you know as much as possible about them. It's about creating a story and personality for your business they enjoy and appreciate. Also, it's about expanding your reach with your customers so they want to share your story with their friends and family members.

Don't get me wrong, there's a bunch of new stuff you must know when it comes to media, marketing, contacting prospective customers, etc. There may even be a few new opportunities and tools to stay in better touch with your current customers. However, I will caution you rounding up all your customers in a public forum and networking them together with your staff — it can be downright dangerous. Keep in mind anything online is ultimately public. That means your disgruntled former employees, as well as competitors down the street, can find your clients and friends online if you are sloppy enough to round them up in a public forum.

I'm going to be sharing with you each month everything new you need to be doing online and in various media. There's a bunch of stuff you must be wary of when it comes to social media and discussion forums. Be eternally vigilant about defending your reputation and managing your "ratings" on Google®, Yelp®, Yahoo®, Bing®, the BBB® and the many other online rating services where anyone can anonymously slam your business or your character.

I'd suggest you start with a couple of "vanity" searches for your name and your business's name in Google, Google Maps, Yahoo, Bing, and Yelp, to see if anyone has rated your business. Take the time to rate yourself a five-star. Get your staff and enthusiastic clients to give you a five-star rating. Keep an eye on each of these regularly. You want to have great customer service. However, there's little you can do about a competitor or a single disgruntled client or staff member posting one or many negative ratings. In most cases, if you get a bunch of positive ratings it will wash out the negative. Most of the various ratings are posted in chronological order. Therefore, the more recent drowns out the past. Keep an eye out next month as we discuss Facebook, the BBB, and the many online ratings and how to position your business properly in each.

Making Direct Mail Work for You, Part 1

There are two types of mailing lists you can buy: "compiled lists" and "response lists."

A compiled list is what most businesses who have had success with direct mail tend to use, including me. A compiled list is typically organized from publicly available data. For instance, a compiled list would be one with an organized sort of recipients, such as:

- Individuals within a 3-mile radius.
- Individuals who own their homes.
- Children three to 12 years of age in households.
- Individuals with incomes of $50,000-plus yearly.

There are many list brokers, but I typically buy lists from InfoUSA, such as those with the sample sort above. They are the largest supplier in the industry for these types of mailing lists. For information, visit InfoUSA.com. Other sources exist which may be as good or better, such as Donnelly.

A response list is a list of individuals who have responded to an offer — either as a prospect or customer. For instance, you can buy the list of subscribers to a magazine or the names of purchasers of any TV infomercial products.

The advantage of a response list is you know the individuals on the list will likely be responsive to a similarly targeted offer. Depending on what your target demographic is, the lists may not be useful as most of these lists are from a nation or international audience, and therefore only includes a limited response from those within a good radius of you and your business. Additionally, the list brokers typically require you to buy a minimum of 5,000 names at a considerably higher cost per name than a compiled list.

You can overcome these challenges by working cooperatively with similar local businesses. For example, if a parent is willing to spend money on upgrading her TV package, then she will also be open to other products and services that will develop her entertainment part of the house. This is just an example, but you really should support other local businesses as they will support you in return.

There are many thousands of lists available for purchase. You can search for them through Standard Rate and Data Service (SRDS). You can subscribe to its lists or search online; however, SRDS's lists are rather expensive, so your best option is probably to visit any major library. Ask any librarian in the reference area for Standard Rate and Data, and then plan to spend several hours there.

After what I've explained above, it's very important not to forget a simple and powerful fact: the best list of all is your business's lead list of people who have expressed an interest in your business by providing contact information on your website, calling you on the phone, registering for a special seminar, and attending a demo, etc.

Your highest priority of the various grassroots marketing efforts you undertake should be to build your mailing list of interested prospects and to make sure you're in front of them when they are ready to "take the plunge" and purchase something from you. That's the group you want to "drip on", with a never-ending series of monthly mailings, and, perhaps, even more frequently during peak seasons.

Making Direct Mail Work for You, Part 2

D uring part one, I recommended the best lists come from your leads or prospects.

What Determines Response?

Your response from any mailing you do on behalf of your business will be directly affected by the following:

1. The list. If you mail to the wrong target audience, then you can't expect many responses, if any.
2. Your direct mail piece is opened. The biggest direct mail hurdle is your piece being placed in the A pile, or the mail considered important enough to be opened. You can help to make sure your piece is opened with a copy on the envelope (i.e., teaser copy, headlines, testimonials, etc.) to make it more innovative and interesting.
3. The headline. If the headline and first sentence of your letter or piece fail to motivate recipients to continue to read, then the letter is a waste of time.
4. The offer. The offer must be both compelling and time-sensitive using an expiration date, limited time only and any other perceived urgency to respond. That way, they rush to get the deal as it's only on for a little while.

Thinking about Response

A successful direct-mail campaign is all about "ROI" (Return on Investment), not Percentage Response Rate. Instead of being concerned about the percentage of responses you are likely to receive or a low-percentage return, focus on your return on investment.

For example, if your average customer value is $2,000 (i.e., how much the average customer will spend at your business during his or her time there). If you decide to place a Val-Pak ad which costs $320, then your ROI is 600% if just one client signs up.

That's a much different way of looking at the value of advertising: 10,000 direct mail pieces may only generate two calls and one client signing up (i.e., a 0.12% response) but your ROI is 600%.

Almost all business owners don't understand the main two distinctions about the use of direct mail.

1. The best way to increase your gross revenue and net income is to learn and implement the methods which result in higher average client value. You must determine how to ask for larger down payments, higher monthly payments, more expensive upgrades — and, of course, client retention.

2. How much you can feel good about spending advertising dollars is in direct proportion to your average customer value. Increasing customer value increases your options to fill your business.

I recommend two programs that will help you learn how to use direct mail more effectively.

1. Dan Kennedy's "*Copywriting Seminar in a Box*". This is a huge program that covers the topic of writing letters and ads more effectively than any others I've seen.

2. Dan Kennedy also offers an excellent introductory program for direct mail follow-up. You can access his "Magnetic Marketing" program.

There are many excellent books on this subject. I recommend Ted Nicholas, Joe Sugarman, Gary Halbert, and John Carlton. Joe Sugarman also wrote an excellent book on infomercials.

Other Suppliers

I regularly use a variety of suppliers for various activities. For postcards, I use Get Members. It provides comprehensive services: design, purchase of the compiled list, printing, assembly/preparation, postage, and fulfillment. The other is 1800postcards.com, which offers quality full-color printing, but not mailing services.

Let's Talk Frankly About Money, Part 1

I know what you may be thinking: "Is it possible to make a big income or even be rich in the business industry?

I'm no different than you. When I graduated from Georgetown University, I put together a business plan and showed it to my first instructors (Gran Moulder and Bob Olinghouse). I was 22 and excited about moving from Washington, D.C., to Denver, Colorado to set up my first business.

I asked Gran for his feedback on my business plan. (At the time, he was president and owner of a family business. Bob, my other instructor even worked for him for a while.) I mistakenly thought as a "real" businessperson/business owner he might give me some useful ideas.

When I asked for his opinion, he was very helpful. Do you know what he said? "You can go to Denver and 'play at this' for a while and then find a real job." This was very helpful feedback about my career objectives. This wasn't the first time I had heard the "How-do-you-expect-to-make-a-living-doing-this?" line, but this time I was informed and prepared enough to ignore it and just execute my plan.

By the way, a few years later Gran came to visit me in Denver. I had a new Corvette and a huge house on the side of a mountain overlooking Denver. I had 1,500-plus active clients in five locations. I made him "eat crow" although I felt bad about it later when I learned his family business which was in a "real industry" had folded.

Unfortunately, it has been ingrained in many of us that we've chosen an industry where the love of what we do trumps the fact that we'll probably never make much money doing it. That doesn't mean we can't continue to pursue it and make a living from it.

Many potential small business owners have never been able to move past this early, negative "programming". It may have been drilled into you by teachers, parents, siblings, friends, and even your wife or girlfriend that it's just not possible to make a comparable or better living than the "professionals" (doctor, dentist, lawyer, etc.) in your family or circle of friends.

How do you become rich by running your own business?

Many people have run single locations or small multi-location chains effectively. Others have run bigger organizations: Danny "Tiger" Schulmann, Bill Clark and me. These are individuals who have mastered multiple chain operations and became rich running successful business, while also teaching budding businesspeople how to manage their businesses. I'm sure you would agree they've achieved high income and wealth from running their businesses. I can teach you how to do the same thing.

OK, maybe you acknowledge you can make plenty of money from multiple business operations, but maybe you only want to keep your business small and run things by yourself. So, you might find yourself asking the question: is it possible to run a single business and make a large income?

Certainly, it's very possible. I could list some of our business owners who, by following systems, focusing on priorities and managing their expenses, make very good incomes from one single business. You probably haven't heard of them, however, since they're not in the public eye seeking exposure. By the way, there are many anonymous rich people, but you just don't know them. You don't have to be in the public eye to be a successful, rich businessperson. Some you may know include Keith Hafner, my friend in Ann Arbor, Michigan. I could give you Keith's full background but let me give you just a little snippet. A few years ago, he built his dream house, which is in the range of 8,500 square feet on a beautiful treed lot, with a built-in swimming pool, Jacuzzis, workout room and built-in, massive stereo system throughout the entire house.

He runs a business which makes approximately $100,000 a month in gross revenues with a 50% net for many years and still does a lot of the internal processes and communications with the customers. There are many examples of people who live like that.

Let's Talk Frankly About Money, Part 2

Steve Doyon, my friend in Connecticut, is another anonymous, wealthy business owner you probably don't know. He runs a $1,000,000 per year single-business operation. I could continue about single businesses which are generating huge grosses, but also many that may not gross as much but are running high net profits with proper controls and systems in place.

There are many businesses with which I've personally worked about to grow to $10,000 or more per month net profit. Even in my case, my one remaining corporate business had a net profit last year of more than $90,000, after paying two full-time fully trained employees, running it for more than $100,000 and with almost no involvement from me. I visited the business about seven times last year, did none of the teaching and none of the sales, and, frankly, none of the "grassroots" or on-site marketing either.

So many business owners are hung up on the "history of what they do" and ignore what it takes to be rich. Ask yourself now. When you are in your 60s or 70s, what will be more important to you? The physical specifics of what you did when running your business or the fact you helped thousands of customers with what they wanted to achieve by providing tremendous services and products to them, while you earned a great living, providing for yourself and your family and creating wealth to retire comfortably with whatever toys you desire and knowing your children are well provided for?

Here's a serious question for you: Do you want to be financially successful? To accomplish financial success, you must realize that you must focus on what the market will pay and a system and process which will deliver it most effectively to most people. In my business, we understand the market is not clamoring for any style or methodology but is enthusiastic about the outcomes we've created for our clients. Your long-term career move may be to affiliate with us and leverage a true 'national brand', with systems in place to ensure you're providing the best customer care for your customers.

Let's Talk Frankly About Money, Part 3

My business has created a system which is easy to implement and creates very high-quality products and services for our customers, and frankly, more importantly, we've created a marketing process which will flood your business with customers who want to purchase from you. We've created systems to help you provide the highest possible service with a minimum of headaches and maximum profitability. Look in any career area. Does the number one box office draw at the movies star the most accomplished and technically skilled actor or is he or she skilled, charismatic and marketed well? How about the music? Were Madonna or Britney (and whoever is taking their place) the most accomplished and technically skilled vocalists or have they just tapped into the 'pulse' of what the public wants and been properly packaged and marketed? Surely, there are opera stars or other classical singers with better technical skills in an area the market doesn't want.

Do you think Dr. Phil is the most capable psychologist or was he just a genius at packaging and marketing what the public wanted? Does he do much better than the psychologists who aren't willing to market themselves? I'll bet there's a bunch of Harvard-trained 'traditionalist' psychologists upset about him 'commercializing' psychology. That's right, they don't understand either. It's not about being right; it's about capturing the public's imagination and creating a powerful brand that satisfies their needs. Dr. Phil will have a much more powerful influence on the millions of people who learn from him, than the trickle of patients the pissed-off psychologists will help during their careers.

Before you become self-righteous and think I'm talking about diluting the arts and 'selling out' on quality, let me share with you a quote from Paul McCartney: "Somebody said to me, 'The Beatles were anti-materialistic.' That's a huge myth. John Lennon and I used to sit down and say, 'Now, let's write a swimming pool.'"

That's a quote from the most covered band of all time, which is still one of the most popular and profitable bands ever — more than 30 years after they disbanded. There's even a Cirque Du Soleil show of all Beatles songs. Regarding Paul McCartney, if you don't know, he's considered the most successful pop composer of all time. In the Guinness Book of World Records, he is cited for the most records sold, most number one records (shared) and the largest paid audience for a concert (350,000-plus people, 1989 in Brazil).

If Lennon/McCartney can become the most respected songwriting team in history by focusing not just on the 'purity of their craft', but also on 'let's write a swimming pool', then don't you think you should give yourself the right to be rich doing what you love and creating great results for your clients.

In closing? It's amazing to me so many people (including and maybe especially many in the business industry) ignore the great quote of Zig Ziglar's:

"You have to BE and DO before you can HAVE."

Don't misunderstand me; I'm all about skipping as many rungs as possible to leap to the top of the ladder of success, but many basics must be addressed to reach the top rung and stay there. Ultimately, your long-term success is all about character. You must combine a thirst for knowledge and a willingness to implement aggressively and try new things. Recently, I seem to have been surrounded by two types of losers, who will always remain losers until they reorient their worldview.

Type #1: "Win a Little Bit and Quit". I've seen multiple business owners recently implement a couple of ideas. Their grosses jump from $10,000 to $12,000 per month; their nets jump $5,000 to $7,000 a month, and then just quit. They've decided this new (rather mediocre) status quo is everything they ever wanted and more.

Certainly, it's great to move from near insolvency to a $75,000- to $120,000-a-year income but achieving that goal first is much easier than maintaining it month after month, year after year. Second, the habits and actions a business owner learns when almost insolvent don't support him well to the next level of success and, often, after an immediate flush of success, come back to haunt him. Finally, the next step is achieving these results through others — consistently. That's much harder than it looks and has some ups and downs.

Type #2: The "Magic Pixie Dust" crowd. They lament: "Gee, this is too hard; I must work too many hours. Why can't you just do it for me and send me the deposits while I sit on my couch and watch American Idol?"

Some people watch my business from afar and conclude they can take a few ideas and essentially — overnight — run their businesses by remote control. Interestingly, the ones who seem to whine the most are the 25 to the 35-year-old crowd; it's members who have barely started their careers!

Frankly, the reality is most 'overnight' successes I have ever known, have worked, learned, experimented and thought about their business 24/7 for many years before being recognized as an overnight success.

I can teach you to progress from a $50,000-a-year income to a $125,000-a-year income — then to double that to $300,000-plus, then to double that again to $600,000, but only if you are willing to keep growing — and work hard. Remember, the skills and thinking which took you to your current level of success are different from the skills and mindset which will move you to the next level.

A Reveal of Ten Mistakes You Might Be Making

Toby and I just returned from the Financial Power Summit in Dallas, Texas. I'm honored to be joined on this tour by Grandmaster Y.K. Kim, Master Kirk Pelt, and Master Keith Winkle. Other than the fact my entire family ended up sick a few days before the event, myself included and I ended up putting on my game face with a serious virus; the event was fabulous. I have some takeaways from the event and some observations I'd like to share; it was interesting. Bob Dunne, Toby Milroy and I went about really investigating everyone who was preregistered for the event. I reviewed everyone's website. Toby and Bob called all the businesses to do info-calls on them.

I intended to play the audio of the calls and review the websites during the event. Toby hyperventilated on that one — sure I was going to offend everyone before the session even got going. I'm not sure I have the numbers exactly right, but on the calls, it was something like 20 calls placed, 17 "no" answers and 3 answered "yes". Two of those three ended up chasing down a "rat hole", discussing the merits of their various styles and programs and not asking for a name, number, and appointment. Embarrassing. I explained these are among other things I've tracked for years when information calls come into our businesses.

I will tell you the websites were scary, with a couple being mediocre — the rest of the websites were just horrible. They missed key points I've been doing for years. They mostly spent a ton of time talking about their style and their biography. I irritated a few in the seminar by pointing out that no one cares. The customer wants to hear about benefits, feedback from other customers and have an easy way to learn more.

In almost every case they made no effort to capture information. Just about everyone confuses stuff that may be useful for their current customers with information for prospective customers. At the very least, you want a clear path for prospects to learn about the benefits of your business and to raise their hand to learn more.

I walked through with one member looking at her website. My comment was first: Who are your customers? Answer: mostly kids (60 percent kids, 40 percent adults). About half of the adults came in with their kids. If that's true, then my point was to look at your website from the perspective of a "soccer mom" of a seven-year-old girl. What does that mom think about the patch with a knife and sword? How about the photo of two kids sparring with one kicking the other in the knee?

You get the picture. You've got to look at it from the perspective of your prospective customer who knows little about your business but wants to know more. Look at it from the perspective of the potential customer. Forget your preconceptions and look at it from the standpoint of a new prospect.

Another observation from the event. About half of the people in the room were from businesses in the $5,000 per month range or less. The other half was in the $20,000 to $40,000 per month range. I told one of them the areas where he was screwing up were the areas where he was resisting what his organization was telling him to do, clinging to a variety of irrelevant services and products and maintaining a shadow website which didn't follow the organization's recommendations.

As usual, those who made the effort to hog time, tell everyone about their great ideas and argue simple points, were the business owners doing $5,000 or less per month. I was unusually diplomatic (for me) but, frankly, it gets annoying listening to failing business owners share their secrets of failure. These failing business owners are clear the success skills shared won't work in their community, with their clients, with their style (as if any of that matters). The business owners in the room doing the best — the top 10% guys — were sitting on the edge of their seat, taking notes — in some cases brought an audio or video recorder — and asked specific, directed questions to have an action plan. I'd certainly like to express appreciation to the members who attended and contributed, so thank you. After the seminar, I took the time to do more thorough evaluations. In one case for a business doing $4,500 to $5,000 per month, it didn't take long to find the problem areas.

The quick list:

- No organized info call, introductory offer or process.
- No contracts, strictly month-to-month.
- No outsourcing or automating billing. Having customers bring checks in every month for payment.
- A poorly designed structure, with no down payment to get started.
- An average monthly customer value that wa too low.
- No renewal program (or 'upgrade').
- Complicated business structure.
- A predisposition about what their customers and prospective customers will and won't do.

A near-total reliance on 'word of mouth' for new clients without a real referral system.

I don't have the space to go into all these items here. I will tell you members who have poor results focus primarily on learning new 'stuff' from the materials we share and don't pay attention to the monthly tele-coaching calls and fail to study the material in their monthly "Maximum Impact" package. Developing new skills is vital, and you must have a focused approach to generating new clients and creating maximum client value. To thrive, you need to focus on fabulous customer service; make sure you have a clear and effective sales process in place for prospective customers and renewals and keep your pipeline filled with new clients.

On the billing side, I'll tell you I don't have a 'dog in this hunt'. What you must do is require all payments be automatic through EFT or credit card. You can automate that with software applications, or you can hire a billing company. Don't be "penny wise and pound foolish" on stuff like this. Hire an accounting firm, payroll service firm and automate or outsource your billing.

I will leave you with one thought. There's no excuse for having fewer than 100 clients grossing less than $20,000 a month. Every business I've ever opened was at 100 or more clients in the first six weeks. If you are running a small business full-time, plan and add 100 clients in the next 60 to 90 days. It's completely doable. You may spend 20, 30 or even 40 hours a week 'beating the bushes' for new clients. I will tell you working hard is a hell of a lot better than being lazy and broke. Frankly, you may have to work hard on your marketing to build momentum, but it's a lot easier to keep business rolling than to get it there in the first place.

Another point many miss out is that no matter how many 'referral systems' you have in place, it's tough to grow from within when you have a small number of customers. You've got to jump-start things with community outreach and advertising. In the early days, most of what I accomplished was through pure manual labor. It's easier to spend a big stack of money to fill your client, but it's just about making a decision and getting to work.

7 Steps to a Flood of New Traffic

I just returned from a couple of days in our business in Fresno, California. It was a great experience, and there were lots of fabulous clients. The employees were very motivated and energized — you could feel it when you walked into the building. Their new monthly records being hit and overall, there was great momentum in the coming year. They were flooded with introductory traffic. Most of what I was working on was improving ratios that have slipped due to volume and renewal ratios.

In working with them — with a target of really being a million-dollar-a-year business by the end of the year — I reviewed our standard approach to going from mediocre to fantastic.

First step: fix processes and systems. Look at your monthly retention rate and reduce your monthly dropout rate to less than 3% of your active clients. If it's 5% or above you've got to figure out where the problem lies. If you have a problem, it boils down to the quality of the products and services you provide, your employees or the overall customer process. It's important to chunk it down appropriately.

To improve your retention, take a look at a couple of important considerations.

1. The first few months are only about getting the client committed. Help them have success. If they feel successful, then they will want to try your services and products again.
2. Make sure there is a regular process. If the client is concerned about anything to do with their purchases, ensure you have a process in place to help them where it's needed.
3. Make sure you hire staff who are more concerned about their clients than themselves. Those who are well trained and have a genuine interest in making their customers happy are the ones you should aim to have. Many of us make the mistake of hiring staff based upon talent, but it's empathy and sincere concern for your clients that is more important.
4. Keep track. What gets measured gets done. Pay close attention to

the inner running of the business; which clients are voicing complaints; which ones are thinking of downgrading their service or quitting completely; which ones are upgrading etc. The point is you must make a huge effort to retain your customers and ensure they renew year after year. Track this, know what your average loss of customers and try to figure out if there's any pattern to it.

Ultimately, client retention is more about rapport and sincere concern for your clients and less about what you can offer them. If you like your clients, know who they are and remember their goals and needs, then they will like you and know you are sincere.

Second step: fix your pricing. You should be charging enough per month for new clients, though this does depend on what industry you're in and what service you are providing them. Typically, you can have upgrade options on your services and subscriptions, where the price can increase by 50% to 100% or more. I typically have an option that's double and an option that's a 50% increase. Again, we've seen businesses that don't use contracts. I believe your initial contract should be approximately six to 12 months.

Hands up, I'm a broken record on this: *it doesn't matter* what your competition is charging. Your prices can be more than double of anyone else in town — if you are marketing properly — and it won't make any difference. My studies show less than 5% of prospective clients ever shop at other businesses. Frankly, some businesses are so bad that if you have an amazing team of employees on hand to help, proper structures and processes, as well as a good quality product or service on top of that, it won't make any difference anyway. Much of what we teach is 'marketing in a vacuum'. They should be deciding if they like what you offer or not. Then they'll decide if they can afford it or not. Your real competition is another discretionary spending, other sports activities, and other developmental activities.

Third step: fix your ratios. Get your contact (info call or lead call)-to-appointment ratio right: 70% or 80% introductory to full customer ratio in place.

Fourth Step: fill your pipeline. Flood your business with new prospective customers. There are many ways to do this, but I'll tell you it's simple — perhaps not easy, but it's simple. You've got to work hard, beat the bushes, get out in the community, network with clients — but it's simple, so remember that.

Back to Fresno: they've generated 248 leads (contact with name, address, phone, email that expressed interest) in the last two weeks. They've scheduled 148 appointments and have acquired 14 of them so far as customers. They are on track for 40 new customers this month at $400 down and $197 a month on a 12-month contract.

There are many ways to fill your pipeline. Most take time, money or both. In their case, they've been making a bunch of appointments at carnivals, fairs, and other community events. Every business should be working on public relations, community outreach, internal events, and advertising every month. You really must plan on spending most of your time out in your community finding prospective clients until you get to 250 or so who are active and paying. You've got to continually beat the bushes and fill your pipeline.

Fifth Step: once you've flooded your sales pipeline with prospects, go back to step three and fix your ratios — again. With volume, things start getting sloppy. You've got to step back and fix those ratios, keep them tight, even with 100-plus new customers per month.

Sixth Step: review your new products and services, making sure they are fabulous. Build up the hype around the new things you can offer through marketing.

Seventh Step: take a look at your upgrade ratios. I want to target 75% of your new clients ending up in your next level in the first four months. Our target is 50% of new clients renewed in the first two months, 50% of those left renewed within the next two months.

You may need to reframe your perspective on this. The best way to improve your retention is to improve your renewal ratios. If they don't renew, they are going to drop out. If you renew them early when they are ready, your ratios will improve.

An important note: It's essential to renew them when they are ready. If they don't renew when they are ready, they may never renew. Also, don't push them too hard to renew. Jeff Smith's analogy is that it's like buying a watermelon. You thump them to see if they are ripe. Once ripe, it's time to renew. You never wait until the end of the year to renew someone for a year. Frankly, in the early months of their lessons is when you must prep them for long-term follow-through. If you don't do it then, it will likely never happen.

Positive Reviews from Readers About The Way of The Mile High Maverick

"If you want insight into what the top 1% are doing and thinking, get the book. It represents the 'cutting edge' of successful small business systems along with the various perspectives, attitudes and techniques that support those systems. The information applies to ALL types of small businesses and practices.

"I personally enjoy and agree with Mr. Oliver's perspectives but, for many it will require a significant paradigm shift toward doing what is best for your clients, your team, and your community. That is the 'gateless gate' that many business owners will fail to pass, resulting in failure to achieve the full potential of your practice for your clients and community. Get the book, avoid these common mistakes, and reach your full potential!"

David Arnebeck

"As someone who grew up working with Stephen Oliver and had the opportunity to know him as both an instructor, employer, business owner, and mentor I can tell you first hand he knows what he is talking about. In my 25 years as a part of his organization, I have experienced first-hand the dramatic effects of what Stephen Oliver's business models can do for new businesses, and established businesses alike. I have seen him walk into businesses with 20 clients and within weeks have the business flooded with hundreds of new clients.

One of the things I appreciate most about Stephen Oliver, is his fresh but historical perspective on the martial arts industry as a whole. He has captured that perspective, along with a blast of sometimes brutal honesty in his new book The Way of The Mile High Maverick. *Every chapter has insights and benefits that will help both novice and experienced businessowners alike. I would highly recommend this book to anyone and everyone in the martial arts industry looking to move to the next level.*

Korey and Sara Stites, Wheat Ridge, CO

"The strategies that Stephen shares and at times 'pounds in' will resonate well for both martial arts businessowners and entrepreneurs alike. The Way of Mile High Maverick is a playbook for those not only looking to improve not only their bottom line, but the concepts he stresses will successfully take any business to the next level."

Don Southerton, CEO
Bridging Culture Worldwide
and Author

"Stephen Oliver is the hidden genius behind some of the most successful practices and small businesses in the world. He's become the 'go-to' consultant for the very top tier to take them to the next level of profitability while showing them how to improve their life-style in the process. I've known him for over 15 years and have seen him in action. He's the 'Real Deal' — straightforward, at times even brutally so.

I'd highly recommend his latest book: The Way of The Mile High Maverick *as a rare peak behind the curtain to help you jump your business into the top 10% or, even 1% of your Industry. I promise you this book will shave years off your learning curve!"*

Lee Milteer
Author of *Success Is an Inside Job*;
Millionaire Smarts Coach
www.milteer.com

"I HATE, HATE, HATE it … when one of my competitors produces an incredible resource. I read Stephen Oliver's The Way of the Mile High Maverick *and was blown away by his content, insight and 'just tell it how it is' style, complete with facts and figures. This is an absolute MUST read for EVERY Businessowner out there. I hate to admit it but it is GREAT! Get and read this book NOW!*

Congratulations to Stephen Oliver on a great job very well done!"

Leigh Childs, The MA Success Guy

163

"I just read Stephen's new book, The Way of The Mile High Maverick. Great book! It is a great resource for anyone to grow their practice or business.

I especially liked the sections talking about ethics and "walking the walk." For everyone, I liked the chapter "The 10 Secrets of Leadership."

There are tons of valuable strategies for the old timers and for those who are new to running a business. If you are thinking about opening a practice or if you have been around for years, this is a must for you. As it mentions in "Mile High Maverick," NEVER stop learning.

One last point: 'Why reinvent the wheel?' Get the book and take advantage of those who have years of experience in business and are willing to share it with others."

Pat Worley
USA Karate, Inc.
Minneapolis-St. Paul

"I've known Stephen Oliver for over 40 years. It's amazing to have watched his growth in our industry. He's now the 'Go To' expert for all of the veterans like myself who would have thought there might not be anything left to learn as well as the 'Young Guns' who are in the top 1%, or top 5% of businessowners. He's the guy who stays at the 'Leading Edge' of what's REALLY working today — and, I guarantee you he'll be the first to use and share each of the new tools that come available.

If you are successful in our industry, you're probably already working with him, if not you should be. If you are planning on 'making your mark' in your industry, Stephen's the only Business Consultant to get you into the very top rungs!

Jeff Smith

"When people ask me how to advance, I always give the same suggestion: 'Find someone who has mastered what you want to do, and then find a way to learn their secrets.' You believe you have the ability to support and treat your clients well, and you believe you have the duty to prosper to where you live with dignity and the financial power to permit your family to follow their dreams too? Find u master who has done what *you dream of doing and learn the tested secrets.*

"My friend Stephen Oliver is one such master who has invested years to build and test his program for creating small business success. Get his book and study it, and pay attention to any ideas that cause you to balk or resist; that is where you need to upgrade your thinking to get bigger better results. Stephen Oliver shares lots of good secrets and guides you through the confusion to help you build success."

Stephen K. Hayes
Black Belt Hall of Fame
Author of 20 books on martial and meditation traditions of Japan
www.StephenKHayes.com

"OK, I am blown away with the content of your book. There is so much. I need to study all of it! God Bless You and Thank You. I do not think there is another publication out there that can come close to your book!"
Keith Joseph Bennett

"Just finished Steve's new book. Must read for everyone in the biz. Jump to the chapter on leadership first then go back and read the rest. Fast read worth the time spent. Many hidden ideas inside. Take notes while you read."

Bill Clark

"Stephen Oliver is the 'Maverick of Business Success." His book is inspirational!"

John Chung

"If you play at running your practice and are fed up with playing and you are ready to take your business to the next level, there is no other choice but the one. If you do not know who the one is that's OK. Read his book The Way of The Mile High Maverick and you too will be the 1.... The top 1% that is. I have lingered in the lower 90% for six years thinking I knew the answer; After all, I am great at the technical aspects of my practice. Thanks to Stephen Oliver I learned that you can be the best technician in the world but that does not mean you will be a great business owner. Bottom line: With this man's expertise and help, along with this amazing

book, I know I am we'll on my way to joining him in the top 1%. Will you join me? Worth its weight in gold!

Adam DiStefano

"Stephen Oliver has set the standard in true consulting professionalism. I have known Mr. Oliver for three decades and he had my attention when he produced a national event, but it was behind the scenes that really impress me. His organizational skills are the standards for some in the industry, he is my friend and fellow professional who will be continually be in the eyes of our industry for progressive progress in the business world. He is 'a Professional Maximizer."

Professor Gary Lee

"History allows us to take a step back and evaluate the impact of those before us. It opens our eyes to disappointments but it also reveals pathways to success. Our business has a unique history going back to its roots and extending itself to the rest of the world. As it spread across the country, it has changed, recreated itself many times and continues to evolve; and such is the case for today's small businesses.

Gone are the days of just asking for a referral, today we have the Internet, social media and a variety of ways to bring awareness to our practice. Stephen Oliver is not only a man who has had his share of battles, but has proven to overcome all obstacles and establish one of the most successful businesses in our industry today.

In an effort to share his methodology of building a more successful business environment, he has created a more comprehensive approach at bringing the modern day businessowner into this new era of social media. In this new book, he provides a unique way of examining our own history and taking our passion into a more rewarding and even profitable industry. The world has changed and so must our practice. I found this book to be very encouraging.

It is not a how-to book, but a book on philosophy and reshaping our mindset to make a successful living on something we love. Stephen doesn't hold back, he says it like it is, and if you can keep an open mind and not get offended, he provides a series of concepts that will have an immediate and direct effect on business enrollment, a more improved working environment and a pathway to running a more successful practice.

Michael Matsuda

"Thank you for allowing me an advance look at your latest book. I simply couldn't put it down, and although I have followed the teachings of the "Mile High Maverick" for 8 years now, this book will be read and re-read as are your other publications. Your absolute clarity and clear road map to success have seen the quality of our clients, the standard of our practice and my family's financial security take massive leaps forward.

Having previously been at the top of the industry in New Zealand, I traveled to the USA in 2006 looking for the next step.

With my oldest daughter in my business and three more about to start I knew I had to find the best I could for them. Attending your Extreme Success event, I learned more about client service and running a business in two days than I had in the previous twenty years — and I had tried many avenues.

I couldn't believe here was the opportunity to go straight to the top of the Industry.

I have since brought my own Instructor into MHK in what is the true full circle we often speak of in the arts. Any Practice Owner who wants to improve their impact in their community — dramatically improve the quality of their service to create a prosperous and secure financial future for themselves and their families — must get connected with you either via your books, your coaching or your live events.

Your knowledge is universal as evidenced by our success in New Zealand, obviously a long way from the States. Again, thank you for your contribution to our Industry.

No one know where a teachers influence ends."

Grant Buchanan
New Zealand

"Stephen Oliver is without a doubt one of our industry leaders in outstanding client service with tried and true business skills. This book is a must in recommended reading for anyone considering opening up a successful practice!"

Karen Eden

"Ignorance is not bliss, it's torture. I didn't know what I didn't know, once I read this book — The Way of the Mile High Maverick — I realized how deep the rabbit hole goes. This book is the tipping point from mediocrity to excellence in small business management, comprehensive, thorough and to the point. Beware, a read through means you can no longer use the excuse, 'I didn't know.'"

Peter Johnson

I found Stephen Oliver's new book very interesting. I have been doing this a long time, but I found this book fantastic reading. Stephen has great ideas and knows how to put them to use. I highly recommend his book and I believe that you will see results immediately."

Bill "Superfoot" Wallace

"Stephen Oliver and I have been close friends since the early 1980's. Been through a lot together. I count him among my closest friends."

"And yet, reading his latest book, The Way of the Mile High Maverick, left me boiling mad!"

"Wanna know why? Because each time I turn a page, I find myself saying, 'I WISH I HAD WRITTEN THAT!!!!' "

"Nobody -- and I mean nobody — shoots straight the way Stephen Oliver does."

"Straight talk. Without apology. So straight, at times, that faint hearted, timid readers might feel like they've been gut-punched. I can just hear Stephen saying, 'Tough! This isn't for you, anyway!' "

"If you are a serious entrepreneur; if you are totally committed to building a financial future for you and your family...do this, right away: Take the mushy, touchy-feely business books you've been reading and throw them in the garbage. Then, us fast as you can, get Master Oliver's book."

"Next. Go home and lock the doors. Turn the phone off. And don't leave your home until you own each one of these powerful lessons."

"If you can't use the information to reach your personal and financial goals...you might as well close your business and take the safe job your family thought you should have taken in the first place!

Keith Hafner, Ann Arbor, Michigan

"Our industry has been waiting a long time for a genius visionary like Stephen Oliver! He is the greatest, most knowledgeable role-model for the modern-day Business professional. Every businessowner MUST READ this motivational, inspirational and educational guidebook for success! This book will take your business three steps higher by skyrocketing your income, enrollment, retention and reputation."

Y. K. Kim
Best-Selling Author

"Stephen Oliver is on the cutting edge of modern business. His new book combines decades of focused experience with exceptional business insight to share the secrets to building a multi-million-dollar empire. If you want to create a successful future for yourself and your clients, you can't miss The Mile High Maverick!"

Kirk Pelt
President of MAW, Inc.

Made in the USA
Columbia, SC
25 February 2023

12925738R00102